# ANTITRUST
AND THE BOUNDS OF POWER

# ANTITRUST AND THE BOUNDS OF POWER

The dilemma of liberal democracy in the history of the market

───

GIULIANO AMATO

HART PUBLISHING
OXFORD
1997

Hart Publishing
Oxford
UK

Distribution in the United States by
Northwestern University Press, 625 Colfax, Evanston,
Illinois, USA

© Giuliano Amato 1997

Hart Publishing is a specialist legal publisher based in Oxford,
England. To order further copies of this book or to request a list
of other publications please write to:

Hart Publishing, 19 Whitehouse Road, Oxford, OX1 4PA
Telephone +44 (0)1865 434459 or Fax: (0)1865 794882
e-mail: hartpub@janep.demon.co.uk

British Library Cataloguing in Publication Data
Data Available
ISBN 1–901362–29–9 (hb)

Typeset in 12pt Bembo
by SetAll, Abingdon
Printed in Great Britain on acid-free paper
by Biddles Ltd, Guildford and King's Lynn

# CONTENTS

*Preface* vii
*Table of Cases* ix
*Table of Legislation* xiii

Antitrust: Introduction 1
    On the surface—the technical profiles 1
    In the foundations: the dilemma of liberal democracy 2

## Part I   Technical Profiles: the USA

1. Protection of competition or of freedom of contract? 7
    From the common law to the Sherman Act 7
    Early years of the Sherman Act 10
    Prohibitions to protect market pluralism increase 14

2. Today's Subtle Weapons 20
    The Chicago School 20
    Evolution in the Supreme Court 24
    Trends in recent cases 27
    The present position in summary 33

## Part II   Technical Profiles: Europe

3. The Heritage of History 39
    Europe's industrial culture 39
    The Freiburger Ordoliberalen School 40
    Early development of antitrust law 41
    Antitrust in the European Community 43

## CONTENTS

### 4. "Restrictive" Agreements — 46
- The normative machinery — 46
- Vertical agreements — 47
- Horizontal agreements — 54

### 5. Abuse of a Dominant Position — 65
- "Special responsibility" — 65
- Assessment of "dominant position" — 67
- Abuse as an "objective concept" — 69
- Individual types of abuse — 72
- In conclusion — 76

### 6. Prohibitions of Dominant Position — 78
- Mergers: the ban and its limits — 78
- Antitrust against public monopolies — 88

## Part III  Antitrust and the Bounds of Power

### 7. Drawing together the threads — 95
- Original aims and later evolution — 95
- In the USA — 96
- In Europe — 98
- The limits to antitrust law — 100
- Facing concentrated, competitive firms — 102
- Changing markets—what remains? — 105

### 8. The Dilemma of Liberal Democracy — 109
- The dilemma of liberal democracy within the dilemma of efficiency — 109
- Towards autonomy of European antitrust from other common policies — 113
- The global market and tomorrow's antitrust — 124

*Index* — 130

# PREFACE

THIS work arises from a seminar I led on the same topic at the European University Institute, Florence, and at New York University, there together with Professor Eleanor Fox. The text is thus an unwinding of the guiding thread of that seminar, and the range of cases dealt with (certainly not the outcome of systematic selection) is what was used for the seminar, in relation to discussions with the students. In reviewing American and European antitrust development, the more analytic treatment has been given the latter, as being less well known on either side of the ocean.

I am very grateful to Ian L. Fraser, who has translated the initial Italian draft and made the text sometimes clearer in English than it was in Italian.

# TABLE OF CASES

A. Ahlstroem Osakeyhitioe and others v. Commission
[1994] 4 C.M.L.R. ............................................407, 57
A.B. Volvo v. Erik Veng (U.K.) Ltd. [1989]
4 CMLR ......................................................122, 90
Aerospatiale/Alenia/De Havilland, Case No. IV/M.053,
1991..........................................................................83
AKZO Chemie BV v. Commission [1993] CMLR 215 ....71
Alcatel/Telettra, Case No.IV/M.042, 1991 ..................82
Appalachian Coals Inc. v United States 288 US 344,
(1933) ....................................................................14
Asia Motor France & Ors. v. Commission, 1996
ECR II-961 (T387/94)............................................122
Aspen Skiing Co. v. Aspen Highlands Skiing Corp. 472
US 585 (1985)..........................................................69

Berky Photo Inc. v. Eastman Kodak Co. 444 US 1093
(1980) ......................................................73, 112–13
BPB Industries Ltd. & British Gypsum Ltd. v.
Commission [1993] CMLR 32, 70
British Leyland Ltd. v. Commission [1986] ECR 3263, 75
Brooke Group Ltd. v. Brown & Williamson
Tobacco Co. 113 S. Ct. 2578 (1993) ......................71
Brown Shoe Co. v. United States 370 US 294 (1962)....18
Business Electronics Corp. v. Sharp Electronics Corp. 485
US 7171 (1988)..........................................27, 28, 30

Chicago Board of Trade v. United States 246 US 238
(1917) ....................................................................12
Consten and Grundig v. Commission [1996]
CMLR 418 ....................................................48–51, 121

TABLE OF CASES

Continental Can v. Commission [1973]
CMLR 199..................................................................78–9
Continental TV Inc. v. GTE Sylvania Inc. 433 US 36
(1997).................................................................26, 47, 51

Dyestuffs v. Commission [1972] CMLR 557...............54–5

Eastman Kodak Co. v Image Technical Services Inc. 112
S Ct 2072 (1992)..............................................................28–30
Eni/Montedison, Case IV.31.055, in OJ L5/13,
1987......................................................................................64

FTC v. Brown Shoe Co. 384 US 316 (1966)................18
FTC v. Proctor and Gamble 386 US 568 (1967)............19

General Motors Continental v. Commission [1976]
1 CMLR 95.......................................................................75

Hoffman-La Roche v. Commission [1979]
CMLR 211....................................................................70–1, 121

Istituto Chemioterapico Italiano and Commercial
Solvents v. Commission [1974] CMLR 309............73

John Deere Lrd v. Commission [1994] ECR II-957........55

Kali und Salz/MDK/Treuhand N. IV/M.308, 1993.....85
Klaus Hofner & Fritz Elsen v. Macroton GmbH [1991]
4 CMLR 306.....................................................................89

Mannesmann Hoesch, Case No. IV/M. 222, 1992........82
Mannesmann/Vallomer/Illva, Case No. IV/M. 315,
1994......................................................................................82
Matro Hachette v. Commission [1994] ECR II-595......59
MCI Communication Corp. v. AT&T Co. 708 F. 2d
1081 (1983).......................................................................72

Michelin v. Commission [1985] CMLR 282............66, 68
Ministere Public v. Tournier [1991] 4 CMLR 248.........75
Monsanto v. Spray-Rite 465 US 752 (1984) .................35
Muncipality of Almelo v. NV Energiebedriff [1994] ECR
    I-1477...................................................................... 85, 89

Nestle/Perrier, Case No. IV/M. 190, 1992 ................84–5
N.V. L'Oreal and another v. P.V.B.A. De Nieuwe
    AMCK [1980] ECR 3775......................................118

Paulis, E., 119
Pronuptia de Paris GmbH v. Pronuptia de Paris Irnegard
    Schillgalis [1966] CMLR 418............................50–1

Regie des Postes v. Paul Corbeau [1993]
    4 CMLR 621 ........................................................89
Remia BV and others v. Commission [1987]
    1 CMLR 1 ..........................................................122
Rothery Storage & Van Co. v. Atlas Van Lines 792 F 2d
    210, 221 (1986) .....................................................33
RTL/Veronica/Endemol, Case No. IV/M.533, 1995....85

Sergios De Limitis v. Henninger Brau A.G. [1992]
    CMLR 210 ...........................................................51
Societe Nationale des Chemins de Fer Francais & Ors v.
    Commission (T79-80/96)....................................122
Spectrum Sport v. McQuillan 113 S.Ct. 884 (1993).......69

TetraPak Int'l v. Commission [1995] ECR II-762..........70
TetraPak Int'l v. Commission [1996] ECR 1-5951.........73
TetraPak Rausing S.A. v. Commission [1991]
    CMLR 334.......................................................81–2

United States v. Airline Tariff Publishing Co. 1993-2
    Trade Cas. (CCH) para. 70, 409 (DDC 993) .........31
United States v. Aluminium Company of America 148

F2d, 416 (1944)......................................................17
United States v Arnold Schwinn & Co. 388 US 365
    (1967), 25–26....................................................31
United States v. Microsoft Corporation 56 F. 3d 1448
    (1995) ...............................................................32
United States v. Philadelphia National Bank 374 US 321
    (1963) ...............................................................18
United States v. Socony Vacuum Oil Co. 310 US 150
    (1940) ...............................................................14
United States v. Terminal Railroad Ass'n 224 US
    383(1912)..........................................................73
United States v. Topco Assocs. Inc. 405 US 596, 610
    (1972) ...............................................................33
United States v. Trans Missouri Freight Association 166
    US 290 (1897)........................................10–11, 17, 97

Volk v. Establissements J. Veivaecke [1969]
    CMLR 279 .......................................................50

# TABLE OF LEGISLATION

Acts against Restraints of Competition (Germany)....... 128

Celler Kefauver Act 1950............................................... 15
Civil Code 1942 Art. 2616............................................. 40
Clayton Act................................................... 15, 19, 65, 97
   s.7 ............................................................................ 35

Federal Trade Commission Act 1914
   s.5 ............................................................................ 14

Interstate Commerce Act 1887 ....................................... 7
Law No. 834 of 16 July 1992 on consortia (Italy) .......... 40

Regulation No. 2770 of 1972 on specialisation agreements 53
Regulation No. 417 of 1985 on specialisation agree-ments 63
Regulation No. 4087 of 1988 on franchising ................. 51
Regulation No. 4064 of 1989 on mergers ...... 65, 69, 78–9, 81, 84, 87
Regulation No. 151 of 1993 on specialisation agree-ments 63
Robinson Patman Act 1936........................................... 15

Sherman Act ......................................... 8, 13, 30, 40, 96–9
   Art. ............................................................................ 1
   7
   Art. 2 ........................................................................ 7

Treaty of Rome 1950 ................................. 43–4, 65, 119

Treaty of Rome 1950
    Art. 85 ............................. 43, 46–7, 50, 57–61, 117, 118
    Art. 86 ................................................. 73, 74, 79, 118
    Art. 90 ............................................................ 88–9, 90
    Art. 130 ................................................................ 116
    Art. 177 .................................................................. 50
    Art. 222 .................................................................. 88
Treaty on European Union ........................... 45, 116, 118

# ANTITRUST: INTRODUCTION

### ON THE SURFACE—THE TECHNICAL PROFILES

In the book that made him famous, Robert Reich wrote years ago that after decades of intense political importance antitrust had become so technical as now to look like a very private matter for lawyers.[1] There was more than one reason for this disenchantment, the first being the same as had led John Kenneth Galbraith to similar conclusions as long ago as the early 1950s. Faced with the oligopolistic closure of many markets that had come about, the illustrious economist felt that instruments created to guarantee much more competitive patterns had been deprived of their effectiveness.[2]

Undoubtedly there was a bit too much pessimism in that opinion, as was shown by the capacity that antitrust law retained to identify and challenge restrictions on competition in oligopolistic markets, even afterwards. Yet two facts were undeniable. The first was that antitrust law was in any event able to generate increasingly flexible and accommodating solutions. The second was that the underlying problems for which antitrust law had been born were becoming no longer perceptible behind the sophistication of legal arguments and the clash of equally sophisticated economic doctrines such arguments had taken to feeding on, making it still easier for the experts to reach the solutions they did without grasping the meaning of the resulting effects.

---

[1] R. Reich, *The Work of Nations* (Knopf, New York, 1991) p. 39.
[2] J. K. Galbraith, *American Capitalism. The Concept of Countervailing Powers* (Houghton Mifflin, Boston, 1952) Ch. III.

I am writing these candid pages for young people embarking on an immersion in antitrust law, so that, as they become specialists, they will still remain aware of the general issues they ought always to bear in mind. But I am also writing them to remind the experts of the genetic origins of antitrust law; and especially to bring them to a recognition of the traces of that DNA in the complex technical arguments they make choices among in order to resolve dilemmas facing them. For the choices they make do not involve those arguments alone, but continue to find their roots in the great political and philosophical options with which antitrust law still remains bound up.

## IN THE FOUNDATIONS:
## THE DILEMMA OF LIBERAL DEMOCRACY

Antitrust law was, as we know, invented neither by the technicians of commercial law (though they became its first specialists) nor by economists themselves (though they supplied its most solid cultural background). It was instead desired by politicians and (in Europe) by scholars attentive to the pillars of the democratic systems, who saw it as an answer (if not indeed "the" answer) to a crucial problem for democracy: the emergence from the company or firm, as an expression of the fundamental freedom of individuals, of the opposite phenomenon of private power; a power devoid of legitimation and dangerously capable of infringing not just the economic freedom of other private individuals, but also the balance of public decisions exposed to its domineering strength.

On the basis of the principles of liberal democracy, the problem was twofold and constituted a real dilemma. Citizens have the right to have their freedoms acknowledged and to exercise them; but just because they are freedoms they must never become coercion, an imposition on others. Power in liberal democratic societies is, in the public sphere, recognized only in those who hold it legitimately on the basis of law, while, in the private sphere, it does not go beyond the limited prerogatives allotted within the firm to its owner. Beyond these limits, private power in a liberal democracy (by contrast with what had occurred, and continues to occur, in societies of other inspirations) is in principle seen to be abusive, and must be limited so that no-one can take decisions that produce effects on others without their assent being given.

On the basis of the same principles, the power of government exists specifically to guarantee against the emergence of phenomena of that sort; that is, it exists to protect the freedoms of each against the attacks and abuses of others. But this, which is its task, is also its limitation: abuses forbidden for individuals are not allowed for rulers either. Here, then, is the dilemma. How can private power be prevented from becoming a threat to the freedoms of others? But at the same time, how can power conferred on institutions for this purpose be prevented from itself enlarging to the point of destroying the very freedoms it ought to protect?

In a democratic society, then, there are two bounds that should never be crossed: one beyond which the unlegitimated power of individuals arises, the other beyond which legitimate public power becomes illegitimate. Where do these two bounds lie? This is the real nub of the dilemma. Since the existence of these boundaries was pointed out by the first theorists of liberal democracy,[3] there has been

---

[3] "To understand political power aright, and derive it from its original, we must consider, what state men are naturally in, and that is, a state of perfect freedom to order their actions, and dispose of their possessions and persons, as they think fit, within the bounds of the law of nature, without asking leave, or depending upon the will of any other man. A state also of equality, wherein all the power and jurisdiction is reciprocal, no one having more than another". These statements by John Locke, *Two Treatises of Government*, (Peter Laslett, ed.) 2nd edn. (Cambridge, 1967) II, Pt. 4, apart from their author's basic motive of guaranteeing fulfilment of religious duties against any interference,

uninterrupted argument and inexorable division as to where they lie. This division goes back to reasons lying beyond the technical arguments whereby this or that choice is defended in the various areas where the choice has to be made, often in the honest conviction that it is only on these arguments that it can be based. It does not go so far, however, as to reach the idea, foreign to liberal society and yet enthusiastically accepted by many throughout this century, of simply eliminating economic freedom so as, *a priori*, to prevent it degenerating into power. It is a fact that within liberal society itself one of the key divisions of political identity (and hence identification) is between these two sides: the side that fears private power more, and in order to fight it is ready to give more room to the power of government; and the side that fears the expansion of government power more, and is therefore more prepared to tolerate private power.

That was so in the argument between federalists and republicans in the first years of life of the USA and is so today between Republicans and Democrats in the same country. And it is very much so in the division between left and right in Europe, once the layer of Marxism that bore down so much on it in previous decades is scraped off.

In speaking of antitrust law, then, one has also, and primarily, to speak about this crucial and divisive issue. The doctrines that antitrust law has aroused, and the interpretative evolution its rules have undergone and continue to undergo, have been and are a clear testing-ground for the arguments on either side of this division, for both have arguments on their side. The study of antitrust law indeed helps to understand the arguments of each, and to perceive the vitality and meaning of the dilemma that has marked liberal democracy ever since it has existed, and has always run through antitrust law itself.

became the theoretical foundation of liberal democracy and of the concept specific to it of limited power.

# PART I

TECHNICAL PROFILES: THE USA

# 1. PROTECTION OF COMPETITION OR OF FREEDOM OF CONTRACT?

FROM THE COMMON LAW TO THE SHERMAN ACT

The birth of contemporary antitrust law is to be traced back to the USA in 1890, when the US Congress passed the Sherman Act. The law attacked "restraints on trade" resulting from agreements and practices co-ordinated among several firms (Article 1), or from attempts at monopolization by individual firms (Article 2), but from the beginning was given its name "antitrust" because its specific target, most strongly felt at the time, was the increasing use of "trusts" to set prices and divide up markets.

The nascent national American market was emerging from a stage of intense competition among the many corporations that had helped to create it, and the winning firms were seeking instruments to assure themselves of an easier life. The first and most widespread one had been "pooling", a form of agreement in which a "manager" of the pool was entrusted with setting prospective market shares and profit margins. But "pooling" on the one hand quickly came up against the rigours of the law, to the point of being forbidden for railway companies by the 1887 Interstate Commerce Act;[1] on the other, it proved ineffective because the members often yielded to the temptation

---

[1] On "pooling" see, also for further references, E. Fox and L. Sullivan, "Antitrust. Retrospective and Prospective: Where are we coming from? Where are we going to?", in 62 *N.Y.U.L.R.*, 936, 939.

to "wriggle out", and there were no adequate internal instruments of coercion (i.e. there came into being then the "free rider", although the expression was yet to be born). It was John D. Rockefeller who promoted the use of trusts for anti-competitive ends. The trust was a traditional institution of common law whereby one delegated to a trustee *inter alia* one's own right to vote on the board of a company. Through "criss-crossing" voting proxies on their respective boards, the managers of several competing companies together decided price and market policies, each remaining under the control of the others. This created in reality cartels, disguised through the use of trusteeships.

Congress reacted to this in the first place from concern for consumers and for the many smaller businessmen thereby driven out and deprived of their "right to sell". The Sherman Act declared "any" contract in restraint of trade illegal, even with criminal penalties in the most severe cases. However, the law was not entirely innovative in challenging "restraints of trade", but was adapting, amending and disciplining those restraints that had already given rise in common law to rich case law, both in the mother country in England and later in the USA.[2] The difference between the two is of great importance not just in order to understand the meaning of the Supreme Court's first decisions on the Sherman Act, but also for an immediate grasp of the implications in this area of the fundamental principles (and the consequent dilemmas).

What actually was the scope of restraints on trade in common law, and who could either complain of them, or assert them at law? The key point is that in common law the good protected was not competition as we understand

---

[2] See H. Hovenkamp, "The Sherman Act and the Classical Theory of Competition" in (1989) 74 *Iowa L.R.* 1019. A wide selection of relevant cases is in M. Handler, *Trade Regulation. Cases and other Materials* (Foundation Press Brooklin, 1960) p. 104 *et seq.*

it today (since classical economics has explained to us the effects of non-competition on the relation between supply and demand), but freedom of contract in the case of "contracts in restraint of trade", and third parties' freedom (protected against exclusionary practices) in the case of "conspiracies in restraint of trade". In the former case an agreement was, then, restrictive not because it limited competition, but because it limited "unreasonably" the freedom of contract of one of the parties (e.g. by a non-competition clause not ancillary to a sale or to a contract of employment). In the latter case a combination was restrictive when it was so coercive upon third parties as to deprive them of the freedom to stay in the market (a boycott) or to buy goods or services at the best price (a cartel agreement excluding outlets not complying with a fixed price).

The consequences of this approach were twofold. The first was that in order to arrive at breaching freedom of contract an agreement had to impose on the contracting parties themselves obligations that hampered their future contractual freedom. Without such an ultimate effect the agreement was judicially safe, because it was itself an expression of the protected freedom. Similarly, a combination was an illegal conspiracy whenever no alternatives remained to third parties. But a price-fixing agreement, even among potential competitors, was not unlawful whenever the consumer could "walk out of the shop" and buy the same thing from outlets not bound by the agreement (the rule being more rigid only in the sector of prime necessities).

Now comes the second consequence: agreements which were held to be restraints of contractual freedom, and coercive combinations, could obtain no judicial protection, while protection could be secured against them. Non-restrictive and non-coercive agreements nonetheless containing limitations (for instance the obligation to keep to a jointly-set price) on the one hand had no legal protection among the parties, but on the other could not be invalidated in favour of third parties who felt injured by them. It is finally important to note that the conceptual key used to define and distinguish the two types of agreements and combinations was that of "reasonableness". Thus, agreements restricting freedom of contract and coercive conspiracies were unreasonable, but others were reasonable. On this basis, doctrine and case law took it for granted that only "unreasonable" agreements and combinations were impugnable at law, whereas "reasonable" agreements and combinations, even if partially restrictive, were judicially and hence legally irrelevant.

### EARLY YEARS OF THE SHERMAN ACT

The Sherman Act came within this established conceptual and normative pattern, and the attention of those interpreting and defining it immediately concentrated on its opening phrase "any contract in restraint of trade": was it meant really to strike at any restriction, whether reasonable or unreasonable in the common law tradition, or else was it itself established on the old notion of restraint (equalling coercion or violation of contractual freedom), and hence limited to strengthening protection and penalties against agreements (and unilateral actions, through Article 2) that reach the point of being coercive?

Dispute began immediately, based both on the lexicon and on the legislative history. On both sides, arguments were drawn from them for each of the opposing positions. But over and above these arguments, there were points of principle and of the hierarchy of interests at stake, as emerged with full clarity from the Supreme Court's first decisions on the new statute. The most exemplary is perhaps *US* v. *Trans Missouri Freight Association*, from 1897, relating to tariffs established by agreement by an association of (many) railroad companies for transporting freight.[3]

The agreement was a classic pacification after years of intense competition, and the object the companies claimed to be pursuing with it was the interest of users themselves, who through it had reasonable, certain and stable rates, instead of the unpredictable conditions brought by the previous competition that had faced them with never-foreseeable costs.

There is no doubt that on the basis of the common law tradition the "reasonableness" of the restraint would have been more than enough to deprive both users and any possible competitors of protection against it. But the Court took a different view. In doing so, it based itself on a literal interpretation of the statute ("any" contract meant "any" contract, and when Congress had written that it had been well aware of the traditional distinction). Its arguments, however, went much further, maintaining that what was beneficial for users was not the "reasonableness" of the agreed rates, but the dynamics of competition. Nor was it relevant that those rates might even be reduced by an agreement. It was inadmissible for a "combination" to have power over the price and hence to be able to decide the fate of many small dealers, who were instead entitled to their own independence and who from one day to the next might find themselves facing unsustainable costs. Even a competitive market, noted the Court, might also lead to this sort of consequence. But no one could be given the power to bring it about by decision.

The dissenting opinion by Judge White was completely different. To take that view, he said, was to wipe out the "rule of reason", to erase the distinction between reasonable and unreasonable restraints on the basis of which freedom of contract and hence freedom of competition had for

---

[3] *United States v. Trans Missouri Freight Ass'n* 166 US 290 (1897).

decades been exercised. If every restraint was to be regarded as illegitimate and if it was true that every contract always ended up providing for one of some sort, what would become of that freedom? And what of the repeatedly-affirmed principle that when a contract had been freely and voluntarily entered into, it was sacred and was to be respected by every court?

In fact this decision, with other initial decisions by the Supreme Court, went down in history as expressions of a formalistically restrictive approach that saw any restraint as *per se* a breach of the law. It therefore seemed that the Court was contradicting itself and returning to the pre-Sherman Act approach in its decisions a little later when it instead took to assessing the "reasonableness" of the restraints, and accordingly declaring the "reasonable" ones legitimate. This was for instance the case in *Chicago Board of Trade* v. *US*, from 1917, when it accepted the Board's prevention of the purchase of lots of grain, bought at a distance in the afternoon and then sent to Chicago, except at the last price for the morning's dealings.[4] The Court noted that the Board's action was in fact breaking the monopoly power of certain big buyers and warehouses who had exploited the small producers in the countryside by buying up their shipments at distress prices after the close of trade for the day. It thus guaranteed that the latter would be able to sell their grain at the last price that came out of the market.

However, the contradiction with the foregoing decisions is more apparent than real. There is a clear common thread. Both in *Trans Missouri* and in *Chicago Board of Trade* the protection of consumers also implies the protection of small traders or producers, who in both cases are defended from the power of the great. Moreover, over and above the lexical similarity, the distinction between "reasonable"

---

[4] *Chicago Board of Trade* v. *United States* 246 US 238 (1917).

and "unreasonable" restraints now drawn by the Court no longer coincided with the common law one, being instead inspired by a completely new, different conceptual background, supplied by the neo-classical economic theory that Alfred Marshall had begun to spread with his 1890 "Principles".[5] According to that theory, restraint is present and harms competition on the market not when the agreement eliminates someone's freedom, but when it allows the price to be higher than it would have been from the unhampered play of supply and demand; whereas restraint is not present when the agreement gives no one that power, or even takes it away from those who have it.

Looked at this way, it is quite possible to see the two decisions referred to as points on a continuous line seeking to define a new boundary on market power, marked no longer by the alternative between freedom and coercion, but by respect for or distortion of the economic rules laid down for the market itself by the competitive system. In this connection two points should be noted immediately: the first is that the defenders of the old common law boundary see very well that it has now been shifted forward, allowing intrusions on freedom of contract they see as opposed to the very foundations of liberal society. The second is that the progressive emergence of economic theory behind the distinction between "reasonable" and "unreasonable" restraints still does not eliminate restraints that after the Sherman Act were in any case regarded as unreasonable (and were in time to be defined as *per se* illegal), apart from the context and from specific examination of the facts. This was to be true especially for both vertical and horizontal price-fixing agreements, which continued to be seen overall as an attack on freedom and on the market space for the small, and as an unjustifiable distortion of the natural relationship between supply and

---

[5] A. Marshall, *Principles of Economics* (MacMillan, London, New York, 1890).

demand.[6] From this viewpoint, the discontinuity with the common law (which did not offer protection either to price-fixing agreements, or to those who disputed them) was in time to become profound.

## PROHIBITIONS TO PROTECT MARKET PLURALISM INCREASE

For many decades, American antitrust law was to continue building up its edifice on these foundations. It was to have its ups and downs, linked at the same time with political and economic events (after the great depression and all through the 1930s it had to yield more than once to public welfare policies and to the promotion of co-operation and integration among private firms, aimed at overcoming the crisis and remedying what were regarded as the effects of "excessive" competition). But despite that, and despite the progressive reduction in the number of operators on various markets, which therefore took on an increasingly oligopolistic shape, the successive laws went on clarifying what was forbidden and strengthening, to the benefit of market pluralism, the original defence against attempts at monopolization.

By 1914 the Federal Trade Commission Act had been adopted. Section 5 introduced a detailed set of rules against unfair competition, that could also be used (and were actually used later on) to challenge attempts, including unilateral ones, at collusion. The same year had brought the

---

[6] The acquittal of the Chicago Board of Trade does not clash with the unreasonableness, which becomes *"per se"* illegality, of price-fixing. For in this case the Board was applying to afternoon contracts not a price fixed by agreement among its components, but the last price arising from the morning's market negotiations. It was not until later, with the crisis of the 1930s, that the Supreme Court came to tolerate price-fixing in industries in crisis (*Appalachian Coals Inc.* v. *United States* 288 US 344, 1933). Seven years later though, it was to make its *per se* illegality explicit (*United States* v. *Socony Vacuum Oil Co.* 310 US 150 (1940)).

Clayton Act, which was intended to protect small firms against certain coercive and exclusionary practices whenever they "might" lead to a substantial restriction of competition: section 2 had barred price discrimination, section 3 exclusive contracts and "tie-ins", i.e. requiring someone wanting one product to buy another one too (like a photocopier and "its" ink), and section 7 concentrations. Then in 1936 the Robinson Patman Act was enacted, adjusting the discipline of discriminatory prices to the new market situations in which distributors with high contractual power were able to wrest lower prices from producers, securing sometimes unjustified competitive advantages against the smaller. Then in 1950 came the Celler Kefauver Act, amending and extending section 7 of the Clayton Act to include among mergers subject to prohibition not just those resulting from purchase of shares but also those (previously not covered) resulting from direct purchase of the assets of companies. Moreover the new Act covered also the reduction of competition between the merging parties.[7]

In this strengthened normative framework, horizontal agreements, i.e. cartels, continued usually to be prohibited "*per se*"; whereas in relation to vertical agreements, the potential restrictive effect was reviewed whenever they seemed to prejudice the distributor's or the retailer's freedom of resale, on the basis of price freedom. Regarding abusive conduct, from discriminatory practices to coercive contracts, i.e. "tie-ins", bans on them were increasingly to be linked to the market power of the firm adopting them. Accordingly, market power normally came to be the basis for banning mergers regarded as a source of "possible"

---

[7] These were not just technical corrections. Particularly the Clayton Act, but also subsequent laws, gave body to the most conscious reflection in antitrust rules of the defence of the society of equals (endangered by the power of "big business") that lies at the root of American democracy. See R. Hofstadter, *The Age of Reform: from Bryan to F.D.R.* (Vintage Books, New York, 1955).

removal of competition, either because of dominance of the merged firm or foreseeable collusion among the few remaining ones in situations where the entry of new competitors was difficult.

It was mainly the so-called Harvard School that updated the conceptual fabric of antitrust law, fitting into it both anti-competitive behaviour and structures of no longer (or about to be no longer) competitive markets. And the Harvard School was to do so on a partly new basis by comparison with classical economics, namely by grafting onto its essential concepts (demand curve, relation between prices and costs) regularities (and hence rules) derived from analyses of industrial organizations. This was to be the case for the link between "tie-ins" and "leverage", which led to condemning "tie-ins" whenever the firm had market power over the first product and used it as a lever to extend its power to the second one too; and again for the association of the difficulties of entering a market (and hence the definition of its competitiveness) with a single notion of "entry barrier", regarding as such particularly high costs to build plant, or of publicity when the brand had great weight, or a technological gap to bridge.[8]

There is copious case law stretching over many years that uses these concepts and draws on them in the first decades after the Second World War, when industrial growth took off again and traditional fears of concentration that had weakened in the 1930s regained effect. Among the most significant cases in this long, progressive wave, one should first mention *US* v. *Aluminium Company of America (Alcoa)* in which Alcoa's position and conduct were

---

[8] Among the many contributions that started off the School one might read, to understand its methods and approaches, D. Turner, "The Validity of Tying Arrangements under the Antitrust Law" in (1958) 72 *Harvard L.R.* 50; E. Mason, *Economic Concentration and the Monopoly Problem* (Harvard Univ. Press, Cambridge, 1957); C. Kaysen and D. Turner, *Antitrust Policy* (Harvard University Press, 1959).

declared *contra legem* even though, as the sole national producer of raw aluminium it did not incorporate monopoly rent into its prices, and was exposed to competition, albeit largely potential, from imports.[9] The Second Circuit Court of Appeals (in a decision written by Judge Learned Hand) accepted that the imports could set a "ceiling" to Alcoa's prices but added that being subject to a ceiling was not the same thing as being without power over the market (since a six-foot man in an eight-foot room could anyway get closer to the ceiling than a dwarf). Nor was the reasonableness of Alcoa's prices decisive: even a restrictive agreement—as the Court noted, taking up an argument already used in the *Trans Missouri* case in the late nineteenth century—can be reflected in reasonable prices, but does not on that account cease being illegal. What counts is that there is power over the price and, to the extent that is the case, the law's main aim—to keep alive a system of small producers, all independent of each other and not subject to the power of the few—was infringed. The consequence of the argument was that Alcoa was to be condemned for monopolization, not because it had acted with the specific intent to exclude competitors, but for the fact that it had and had used the power to exclude them:

> "It insists that it never excluded competitors. But we can think of no more effective exclusion than progressively to embrace each new opportunity as it opened, and to face every new comer with new capacity already geared into a great organization, having the advantage of experience, trade connections and the elite of personnel. Only in case we interpret 'exclusion' as limited to manoeuvres not honestly industrial but actuated solely by a desire to prevent competition, can such a course, indefatigably pursued, be deemed not 'exclusionary'. So to limit it would in our judgment emasculate the Act; would permit just such consolidations as it was designed to prevent."

[9] 148 F2d, 416 (1944).

Another significant case, a few years later, was *FTC* v. *Brown Shoe Co.*,[10] in which the Federal Trade Commission Act was applied to ban the second national shoe manufacturer from having a "franchising" network of 650 retailers, in the name of consumer freedom to buy on open markets. Meanwhile, in relation to mergers, the Supreme Court explicitly rejected arguments of efficiency, including reduction of costs and prices to the consumer, in the name of the right of smaller operators to compete, which, it said, Congress had wished to protect and it was not for the Court to query. It did so in another case concerning Brown Shoe Co., when in 1955 it merged with its competitor G.R.Kinney, promising a price reduction from the merger.[11] It is true, said the Court, that some effects of these mergers between great chains are beneficial to consumers and are not rendered illegal by the mere fact that small independent businesses may be damaged by them.

"It is competition, not competitors, which the Act protects. But we cannot fail to recognize Congress' desire to protect competition through the protection of viable, small, locally owned business. Congress appreciated that occasional higher costs and prices might result from the maintenance of fragmented industries and markets. It resolved this in favor of decentralization. We must give effect to that decision".

Nor was this an isolated judgment. Again in 1963, in *US* v. *Philadelphia National Bank*,[12] the Court did not even question that the merger would bring the Philadelphia community a bank able to make bigger loans at unchanged rates. But it noted: "Congress proscribed anti-competitive mergers, the benign and the malignant alike, full aware, we must assume, that some price might have to be paid". It was to say the same thing four years later, in *FTC* v. *Procter*

---

[10] F.T.C. v. *Brown Shoe Co.* 384 US 316 (1966).
[11] *Brown Shoe Co.* v. *United States* 370 US 294 (1962).
[12] 374 US 321 (1963).

*and Gamble*.[13] This was, in short, an outright return to the principles of the beginning of the century, to an *a priori* preference for the rights of the smaller, certainly more consistent with the original objectives of the Clayton Act than, in many cases, with the economic analysis, however widely accepted, deriving from Harvard.

According to some, the height of the renewed wave of severe antitrust, after which the wave began to subside along with the traditional fears of concentrations, was the *Kellogg* case, in which the Federal Trade Commission sought to attack the high level of concentration in the ready to eat cereals market, attributing to it a price level that it claimed was higher than costs and asking for the dismantling of the biggest companies. But the attack was not carried through.[14]

---

[13] 386 US 568 (1967).
[14] 99 FTC 8, 267 (1982).

# 2. TODAY'S SUBTLE WEAPONS

### THE CHICAGO SCHOOL

It is always hard to reconstruct the channels, if they really exist, that link the formation of new doctrines, especially those with a high theoretical content, with the evolution of the circumstances they can be applied to; and the pathways leading to the actual application of such doctrines, perhaps after years of purely academic debate, are even more complex. It is a fact that while the wave of expansion just referred to was beginning to swell, around the early 1950s, a professor of Chicago University, Aaron Director, began thinking in depth about individual anti-trust questions, in which he evidently saw traces of a broader common thread. That common thread, highlighted first by him and then by others, became the Chicago School, i.e., the updated, revised return, purged of the Harvard "intrusions" of industrial economics, to the principles of classical economics, which after the late 1970s were largely to overthrow antitrust case law itself.[1]

Director started from the doubts aroused in him by various solutions regarded as accepted. Why should a tie-in be regarded as a means to extend monopoly from one

---

[1] The genesis of the Chicago School is very well recounted by one of its most famous and balanced exponents, R. Posner, "The Chicago School of Antitrust" in (1979) 127 U. of Penn. L.R. 925. The author who ended up most strongly symbolizing it is R. Bork, *The Antitrust Paradox: a Policy at War with Itself* (Basic Books, New York, 1978). Very important is the theoretical contribution by G. Stigler, *The Organisation of Industry* (Univ. of Chicago Press, Chicago, 1968), who traced back to price theory types of behaviour (like collusion) that had been explained differently by industrial economists.

product to another? Usually a tie is not a device likely to produce that result. Not even the monopolist could put the premium both on the tying and the tied products and only one monopoly profit could be taken from the selling. But a businessman is not necessarily so stupid (Director's premise being that the businessman is a rational agent), and it is quite possible that tie-ins are employed for other reasons. Why should predatory prices, i.e. those below cost, be forbidden? The "raider" loses money while practising them, which means he has to raise them again later, if he is not bent on suicide! At that point, once again, there will be room for competition. And again it is worth asking whether the predatory price might not have other reasons. As to markets regarded as plainly uncompetitive, are we sure that the barriers to entry are always really such? The cost of plant, for instance, is the same for the new entrant as it was for the firm already established, and, on the basis of an equal amortization rate, weighs equally on each of them as an annual figure. Why should there be a barrier?

Initially ignored by more accepted scholarship, Director's findings were themselves based on the principles the Chicago School was to articulate later: that, primarily, all that is restrictive in economic terms is only the practice, concerted or unilateral, of restricting at someone's pleasure the production of a good or service, with the consequent possibility of increasing the price, and giving consumers the sole alternative, as they cannot rely on new potential competitors, of having to shift to second-choice goods or services (and this is what encroaches on "consumer welfare"); the principle of the entrepreneur as rational profit maximizer, accordingly acting in ways to be assessed exclusively on an economic basis, beyond any presumptions of short-sighted anti-competitive ends; and the principle that summarized the conclusions the school arrived at, that efficiency is the sole objective of antitrust law, and that what is to be understood as efficient and hence consistent with consumer welfare is any conduct or situation that transfers to the consumer's benefit qualitative improvements in manufacture or in cost reduction, without giving anyone room to "restrict" the market in the sense indicated by the first principle.

The implications of this new approach for the then consolidated interpretation of many antitrust rules were potentially enormous. Vertical agreements almost all became explicable in terms of efficiency, including some of those always regarded as illegal "*per se*" (even including prohibitions on discounts imposed by the manufacturer on the retailer): all could in fact be maintained to be improving the quality of service to customers by sellers, guaranteeing the investments necessary to that end and preventing the ravages of "free riders". Market positions regarded as against the law because of their high degree of concentration became eligible for a contrary assessment whenever the market, even if it had only one operator, could still be challenged because the presumed barriers were not actually such. Only horizontal agreements retained a sort of presumption of illegality, since the requirements for showing their efficiency remained very restrictive. But the Chicago School was always to maintain a certain scepticism about antitrust measures against them too, relying on the cost that complying with cartels always imposes on their members, the resulting temptation to "free riding" within the cartel and the fact that therefore waiting for cartels sooner or later to collapse by themselves always costs less than a long legal case.

This new approach certainly had great merits and an effective capacity to clarify and systematize first and foremost the method of analyzing antitrust matters. But it cannot be said that it was free, whether in principle or in terms of applied solutions, of contradictions, and therefore beyond well-founded questioning and criticism. And criticisms did come. The economic operator is a maximizer of his own profit and it is accordingly right to explain his behaviour primarily on that basis. But this correct methodological choice cannot be converted into an absolute presumption, since often economic operators too are moved by extra-economic reasons (power, rivalry, personal and family prestige) and may ignore costs simply to get rid of a competitor or expand their own business.[2] Moreover, it is true that the consumer of a product or service will likely be pleased to be able to buy it at a lower price and at better quality even from a firm that has eliminated competitors to reach the necessary scale to be able to do so. But can "consumer welfare" be made to coincide with such a restricted concept, ignoring the fact that the consumer might prefer a broader choice of suppliers and that, especially in more innovative areas, innovation and hence quality may be the outcome more of wider competition than of economies of scale by a few already established manufacturers?[3]

Applied solutions were also questioned, and there were not always answers. For instance, it is true that the cost of publicity may be equal for both the established firm and the new entrant, but it is one thing to finance it from the cash flow of an ongoing activity, and another to do so by recourse to the financial market (though here Chicago rightly answered that if there is a barrier it relates to access to that market and to the cost of money). Or again, it is true that those employing predatory prices will then be compelled to raise them, and since antitrust protects not

---

[2] O. Williamson, *Markets and Hierarchies: Analysis and Antitrust Implications* (Free Press, New York, 1975). More generally, D. North, *Institutions, Institutional Change and Economic Performance* (Cambridge Univ. Press, Cambridge, 1990).

[3] E. Fox, "The Modernization of Antitrust: A New Equilibrium", (1980) 66 *Corn. L.R.* 1140, p. 1173. On the relationship between innovation and competition, which in the presence of high costs is the object of polemics that have not been resolved, see J. Kattan, "Antitrust of Technology Joint Ventures: Allocative Efficiency and the Rewards of Innovation", in (1993) 61 *Antitrust L.R.* 936.

existing competitors but competition, one may calmly leave it up to future new entrants to profit tomorrow from that inevitable rise. But are we sure that after one, two or three expulsions of existing competitors by repeated "raids" using predatory prices anyone will dare to put themselves forward?

Let us be quite clear: no criticism, on the theoretical or academic level, has succeeded in dismantling the Chicago School. Over and above its extremisms and its weaknesses, the focus it brought on market power and its demonstration of the efficiency not just of competition but also of many restrictions of competition itself (a much more solid, well-founded basis than the old "reasonableness" for permitted restrictions) have remained acquisitions for everyone. What has to be said is that the success of the Chicago School, which was to reach dizzy heights shortly after 1980, somewhat reduced in most recent years, cannot be explained just by the technical validity of its approach and solutions. We are accordingly brought back to those deeper links that go beyond the technical arguments and must therefore be traced by considering applied antitrust law over the last few decades.

### EVOLUTION IN THE SUPREME COURT

Scholars who like to set changes in case law into the broader framework of overall economic evolution recall that the 1970s were marked by high inflation, the oil crisis, and the first signs of the aggressiveness of Japanese and German products on the American market. Concern at lost competitiveness and jobs and the consequent promotion of policies to strengthen the national industry became crucial, just as had happened in different circumstances and ways during the New Deal.

It was in those years that the Supreme Court's shift in the antitrust area came to fruition; and it came with the explicit entry into its case law of the interpretive principles of the Chicago School, which gave new support first and foremost to the ongoing processes of vertical integration. In 1967 the Court had had to deal with a franchising case in which the Schwinn company, bicycle manufacturer with a strong (even though not dominant) position in the market, had obliged its retailers to sell only to final consumers or else to other retailers tied like them to Schwinn.[4] The restriction of "intra-brand" competition that clauses of this type meant was plain. But it could also be maintained that they were compatible with the offering of service to the customer, and hence with greater competitiveness for Schwinn in the context of continuing "inter-brand" competition. The Court did not however even venture onto this sort of consideration. It declared the restrictions illegitimate *per se*, as violating the retailer's freedom by subjecting him to the manufacturer like an employee. The manufacturer, it said, cannot exercise any power over the resale of goods that have left the sphere of his ownership. These arguments still echoed those in the Court's first decisions inspired by protection of the small operator, which showed traces, to the same end, of freedom of the entrepreneur as an object of legal protection. It is quite clear that on the basis of them there was little room for national firms wishing to adopt more uniformly aggressive policies towards competitors in the distribution network. Respect for competition among distributors themselves was set up as an inviolable obligation.

Eleven years later came the Court's verdict in the case of Sylvania, a TV manufacturer that had lost market (it had gone down to 1 per cent) and in order to climb back had successfully organized (going back up to 5 per cent) a franchising network, with the obligation on retailers in the network to sell only from premises agreed with Sylvania

[4] *United States v. Arnold Schwinn & Co.* 388 US 365 (1967).

itself.[5] The case was similar to *Schwinn*, but could also be distinguished from it: as to the facts, from the absence of any market power for the manufacturer, and as to law because the limits imposed on the retailer here were not on the choice of whom to sell to but only on the places to sell from. Yet the Court felt it necessary to overturn the precedent fully and openly, doing so with due mention of the Chicago doctrine and the scholars who had developed it.

It noted immediately that the impact of vertical restrictions was "complex", since while reducing "intra-brand" competition it could stimulate the "inter-brand" kind. It added that economists had brought out the many ways manufacturers could utilize restrictions of this sort to compete more efficiently among themselves by setting up pre-sale and post-sale services, ensuring maintenance and repairs and protecting the retailers who actually supplied the services from "free rider" retailers operating at cost price. *Schwinn* was overruled. If it was true that restrictions invalid *per se* were ones that were devoid of any "redeeming virtue", while the reasonable ones were those with such virtues, then even restrictions imposed by the manufacturer after the product left his ownership could be shown to have some.

It was just this conclusion that led to the opinion of Justice White, concurring in the result, but dissenting in the motivation. *Schwinn* and *Sylvania*, he said, were cases that could be kept distinct without overruling the first in order to decide the second one differently. Overruling *Schwinn*, said White, meant eliminating the notion that an independent economic operator ought to have freedom of disposal as he wished with goods he had bought. At this point, he added, the very *per se* illegality of vertical price-fixing was in danger, since eliminating all territorial intra-brand competition necessarily eliminates all intra-brand

---

[5] *Continental TV Inc.* v. *GTE Sylvania Inc.* 433 US 36 (1997).

price competition (the first being more restrictive than the latter) and in any case the Chicago economists said that it too should be assessed case by case. Was that where we wanted to get to?

### TRENDS IN RECENT CASES

The Court has never got there, yet in subsequent cases it came close, and even showed glimpses of the new boundary to which the price-fixing bar itself might be shifted. The most exemplary case in this connection is perhaps *Sharp*,[6] decided in 1988 by a majority opinion written by Judge Scalia (a lawyer noted for his conservatism and appointed by President Reagan). Sharp, a well-known electronic equipment company, had listed prices, not binding but only recommended. One of its resellers, BEC, had a very aggressive price policy, to the detriment (among others) of another Sharp reseller, Hartwell, who asked Sharp to terminate the relationship with it on that ground. Sharp (the jury found) terminated the discounter BEC pursuant to its agreement with Hartwell because BEC was a discounter. Was it an "unreasonable" restriction to eliminate a reseller by agreement because of discounts he made?

The Court took a broad approach in its answer. It wrote that there was a general presumption in favour of the criterion of reasonableness in relation to *per se* illegality, and added that the "priority concern" in antitrust was inter-brand competition. On the basis of these premises, in the absence of contrary evidence, it was quite possible that Sharp was pursuing the legitimate objective of securing its resellers the necessary profit for furnishing more efficient services to customers. On the other hand, no agreement setting the resale price or price level had been shown between Sharp and its resellers, and in this connection the

---

[6] *Business Electronics Corp.* v. *Sharp Electronics Corp.* 485 US 7171 (1988).

Court took the opportunity of adding that vertical price-fixing agreements were given rigid treatment by the law as *per se* illegality, particularly because they could be used to form and police a horizontal cartel.

This was the potentially most innovative part of the decision, and it is no coincidence that the dissenting opinion by Judges Stevens and White dwelt at length on the point, rejecting the limitation of the illegality of vertical price-fixing to the situations set forth by Scalia alone, and noting that the reasoning of Scalia logically meant that "*per se*" no longer applied. They further noted that for the first time the justification of efficiency had itself become a presumption, since no evidence had been given of the objects of efficiency that eliminating the reseller, guilty only of applying discounts, was supposed to lead to. But henceforth, on the path of vertical restrictions, the obstacle was almost entirely removed (if there was at any rate the certainty of not weakening inter-brand competition).

It has been asked whether the more recent *Kodak* case[7] marks a return to more traditional positions, or not. That may be suggested by the majority opinion, but not indubitably; in any case there is the very firm, dissenting opinion by Scalia, who would continue to apply to every vertical conduct as to which no power is demonstrated in the inter-brand market, the *per se* legality doctrine set up by him in *Sharp*. What was at issue here was Kodak's behaviour in eliminating organizations of independent operators that previously repaired "its" photocopiers, on the one hand by no longer selling spares outside its own network, and on the other, and consequently, by compelling users to come to its subsidiaries for repairs. Accused of an illegitimate "tie-in" and of attempting to monopolize the market for spares and repairs, Kodak reacted with a principled stance, on the basis of which it asked to be granted a sum-

---

[7] *Eastman Kodak Co. v. Image Technical Services Inc.* 112 S Ct 2072 (1992).

mary judgment, that is, the form of purely legal judgment given prejudicially without even going into consideration of the facts: given that I have no market power over the photocopier market, ran Kodak's argument, that *per se* rules out my having any over the downstream market for spares and repairs; for if I increased my prices excessively in this connection, consumers would stop buying my photocopiers and go to my competitors.

But the Court did not accept the argument and, without going into the facts, referred the matter back to the trial judge to do so, denying the summary judgment. After all, said the Court, it is not true that a price increase downstream necessarily has that consequence upstream, since between the competitive price downstream and the one that manages to turn the photocopier itself out of the market there are always intermediates that can compensate for any fall in sales of the photocopiers themselves. It should further be borne in mind that not all consumers are so sophisticated as to inform themselves before purchase of the cost of subsequent repairs and draw comparisons on that basis; many consumers remain "locked in" after purchase and for them, once the photocopier has been bought, any repair price is preferable to the much higher investment needed to make a change. In any case, and this was the most important argument of principle, even the sector selling spares and repairs for a given machine might be a relevant market, on which, accordingly, a monopoly position could be formed, over and above the inter-brand competition existing on the market for that machine. For anyone who had bought a brand there was no substitutability with parts for other brand machines, and this was enough to shape the market independently in this case (and require verification whether there was competition on it or not).

Scalia's dissenting opinion was as predictable as it was strongly argued: what would have happened had Kodak from the outset, that is, when it sold the copiers, contractually imposed the "tie-in" on its customers? In the absence of market power over copiers, there was no doubt that the Court would have found this tie-in legitimate. Was the judgment to be reversed just because Kodak did it later? But where was the market power? At first sight it might seem to be the kind that Kodak, like any other supplier of machinery and equipment, exercises over those who have bought one of its products. But this is a quite different phenomenon, what Scalia called "circumstantial power", that exists in all competitive markets (from the copier market to the one for refrigerators that work badly) with which antitrust law ought not to deal, since it would otherwise transform section 2 of the Sherman Act "from a specialized mechanism for responding to extraordinary agglomerations of economic power to an all-purpose remedy against run-of-the-mill business torts".

It is easy to understand, then, why the Kodak case aroused so much interest. What is highlighted behind the two positions that emerged is the crucial theme of the different location of the boundary between the risk of too much private power and the risk of too much public power. Meanwhile, at the strictly technical level we will never know how the Court would have solved the case, had it entered into the merit of the facts (which the Court did not) and had it emerged from the facts that the reason for Kodak's conduct was not to get rid of aggressive competitors for repairs, but itself to offer better service, so as better to cope with inter-brand competition on the main market.

In the context of the case, after the referral back to the trial judge, the jury found against Kodak. But as far as the Supreme Court is concerned, it is reasonable to consider that the divergence within it was still the same as with the *Sharp* case. According to the more moderate opinion, the majority in this case, Kodak's efficiency arguments would have to have been proven; according to the more extreme view, in this case the minority, efficiency was to be taken as given. But both accepted that conduct like Kodak's could be legitimate, whereas according to the precedent of *Schwinn*, which can thus be seen abandoned once more, it would have been invalid *per se*.

Faced with this evolution of principles, strongly inspired by the Chicago School, the previous case law tradition stands up better in the area of horizontal agreements, and in some respects also in the area of attempts at monopolization. But the School's influence can be felt here too, in methodological if no other terms. Its constant doubt regarding previously obvious solutions in fact impels verifications of each concrete situation that are no longer allowed to be generic, and must accordingly become increasingly sophisticated. Market analyses are done going well beyond assessing market shares, going into the degree of existing demand and supply elasticity, the foreseeability of new supply, the existence, but also the size, of bottlenecks presented as barriers to entry, expectations of technological and normative innovation—in short, anything that could help towards an effective assessment of possible competition in given conditions. On these more accurate premises, moreover, new interpretive schemes were built up enabling not just the acceptance of situations that previously would have been condemned, but also reasoned strikes against conduct and situations that could previously have been banned only through *per se* invalidity.

At the level of horizontal agreements, parallel price behaviour of a number of airlines, behind which there was no documented agreement, but only continuous exchanges of information among their computer systems, was challenged by the DOJ as a price-fixing agreement and pricing co-ordination, which led to consent decrees that revised the airlines' practices.[8] Disallowed practices of

---

[8] *United States* v. *Airline Tariff Publishing Co.* 1993–2 Trade Cas. (CCH) para. 70, 409 (DDC 1993).

increasing (whether through agreement or unilaterally) one's own market power were extended to include increasing the rivals' costs by, say, exclusionary practices (the stronger firm or firms taking on the best and/or lowest-cost distributors on an exclusive basis, or else, upstream, the raw material suppliers), with the result of getting rid of new entrants without renouncing one's own profit margin even for a short time (by contrast with predatory pricing).[9] It should, finally, be recalled that after a long investigation the Antitrust Division of the Justice Department managed to get a consent decree to stop some of the practices whereby Microsoft was progressively closing the market for software systems, i.e. an obligation to pay Microsoft itself a sum on every computer sold (even if it did not contain its software), an obligation for a minimum of purchases, and in some cases tie-ins with self-restraint obligations: a set of clauses in relation to which, in Microsoft's specific market situation, efficiency did not manage to act as an acceptable excuse.[10]

It is true that in the area of research and development a toilsome turnaround is under way, promoted by the legislature itself, aimed at allowing not just vertical but also horizontal agreements that enable the national industry not to lose ground in technological innovation. But horizontal agreements going beyond research work and reaching into joint manufacture and marketing are still an open issue for courts under the rule of reason and Congress, after removing some legal disincentives to co-operative research in 1984, has not secured a green light as yet.[11]

---

[9] On all this see B. Hawks, "Recent Antitrust Developments in the United States" in the collective volume *Antitrust fra diritto nazionale e diritto comunitario* (Giuffrè, Milano, 1966) pp. 221, 225, with further references.

[10] *United States v. Microsoft Corporation* 56F. 3d 1448 (1995).

[11] Th. Jorde and D. Teece, "Innovation and Co-operation: Implications for Competition and Antitrust", in E. Fox and J. Halverson (eds.), *Collaborations among Competitors: Antitrust Policy and Economics* (ABA 1991) p. 887 *et seq.*

## THE PRESENT POSITION IN SUMMARY

We shall draw the conclusions from this consideration below. For the moment we shall confine ourselves to summarizing what it brings out. American antitrust weapons are becoming increasingly subtle and increasingly in need of analytical support; they are not easy to interpret by non-experts, and moreover affect a more circumscribed area than they once did, even if the blows are still effective. As has been written,[12] the change has been intense, both in lexical tokens and in normative contents: the token "freedom of trade", associated with priority protection for the freedom of the small independent trader, has been replaced by "free rider", associated with the contrary protection of the efficient big manufacturer and big distributor against the free incursions of small independents. While in 1972 a non-competition agreement was invalidated by the Court, even though it was ancillary to a joint venture, for still encroaching on the contracting parties' freedom, in 1986 an agreement of this type had become legitimate, as long as none of the parties had market power and it was therefore explainable as a response to the market: it prevented a "free ride".[13] These were changes of great importance, then, to the significance of which we must return in our conclusion.

It must nonetheless be noted right away that the picture has more than one colour, and that, however circumscribed and rendered almost impenetrable for the broad public by its sophisticated technicalities, American antitrust law is by no means dead. It has shown this by, among other

---

[12] E. Fox and L. Sullivan, "Antitrust. Retrospective and Prospective", cited in Ch. 1, note 1 above, at p. 945.

[13] The cases are cited by E. Fox and L. Sullivan, "Antitrust. Retrospective and Prospective", cited in Ch. 1, note 1 above, at p. 945, n. 51. They are *United States* v. *Topco Assocs.Inc.* 405 US 596, 610 (1972) and *Rothery Storage & Van Co.* v. *Atlas Van Lines* 792 F 2d 210, 221 (1986).

things, surviving (albeit with the changes described) the massive sterilization campaign engaged in for all of its eight years by the Reagan Administration.

That was a commitment manifested along all fronts, from that of investigations and subsequent legal action brought by the Antitrust Division of the Justice Department, to that of legislative initiatives to soften the existing norms.[14] On the first aspect, the fall in numbers of actions brought against presumed restrictive agreements and presumed attempts at monopolization is already indicative: from averages in previous years lying between 15 and 20 cases per year for agreements and always over 10 for attempts at monopolization, down to averages of between one and three in the 1980s. Still more impressive is what happened with mergers, which went up enormously in number and in turnover involved, with exponential growth from year to year: from 2,523 in 1983 to 3,001 in 1985, for values over 40 per cent higher than in the previous year. They included, *inter alia*, the biggest horizontal merger operations in American history, including those of some of the main oil companies (for instance, between Texaco and Getty). Yet in the same years, that is, between 1981 and 1985, the Justice Department queried a total of 28 operations, almost all settled by negotiation with the assumption of (minor) alleviation commitments by the companies involved. Moreover, when the occasion arose, the Administration even made moves to facilitate operations in hand. When Mobil, in 1981, sought to acquire control of Marathon, the Justice Department could not fail to act, because Mobil was then the country's second-biggest oil company and sold to resellers with agreements with its brand only, whereas Marathon was the main independent company, selling to non-tied (and aggressive)

---

[14] The Reagan Administration's (attempted) revolution is recounted by E. Fox and L. Sullivan, cited in Ch. 1, note 1 above, to whom I owe the summary in the text.

resellers. Yet along with the complaint the Department made public an unofficial opinion indicating what partial dismantlings of Marathon would make the operation acceptable.

Nonetheless, in this apparently headlong, unrestrained course, the Administration came up against its strongest restraint: from Congress. Among its supporting initiatives was one to bring in the Justice Department as *amicus curiae* in cases between private parties, alongside the firms accused of restrictive practices. On one of these occasions—the *Monsanto* v. *Spray-Rite*[15] case—the Department invited the Supreme Court to overrule *per se* invalidity of vertical price-fixing. The Court did not in fact address the topic (since the parties had not raised it in the lower courts), but Congress did, approving a budget amendment barring the Justice Department from spending its resources with the objective of altering the *per se* invalidity of price-fixing.

This brings us to the second aspect, namely the attempts to change the legislation, and the fate these met with in Congress. The attempts were bold and wide-ranging: from allowing "criss-cross" management of different companies (recalling the trusts of the beginnings), to authorizing mergers, even though restrictive, that helped to strengthen national industry against imports, to broadly amending section 7 of the Clayton Act in relation to mergers, and even to eliminating (with rare exceptions) "treble damages", the main incentive to private antitrust actions. But Congress dropped all of them, and the attempts failed.

In the long history of American antitrust law, these episodes are by no means irrelevant—especially not the fact that today we can already see as a parenthesis an intense, prolonged commitment to "throwing it on the scrapheap" just a hundred years after its birth. Despite the profound

---

[15] 465 US 752 (1984).

transformation in their case law brought about by the Chicago School, the Supreme Court and the other courts did not support that commitment, but defended antitrust law. So did Congress, though subject to thousands of pressures to protect American industry at a stage—and this too should be recalled—when the USA's decline in the face of Japanese aggressiveness was the hottest topic of debate.

Undoubtedly, though, antitrust law in our day is no longer what it was at the start. Undoubtedly, some of those who theorize its exclusive subservience to efficiency as understood by Chicago include some who have lost all sensitivity to the underlying reasons for it. But the trunk is still living, and we shall have to bear that in mind without any "Manicheism" when we come to drawing conclusions.

# PART II

TECHNICAL PROFILES: EUROPE

# 3. THE HERITAGE OF HISTORY

## EUROPE'S INDUSTRIAL CULTURE

The European story appears radically different in its development. Indeed, its course may even seem to have been an opposite one, since antitrust culture does not go back to our roots but supersedes principles of quite a different kind, and has spread expansively only in the last few years. The increasingly broader area that antitrust law has thus conquered ought not, however, to tempt one down the path of easy conclusions, since the content it has been assuming in Europe, and the assonances and dissonances here by comparison with the developments in the meantime in America, are all things that have to be verified and assessed.

Only Britain, the island which, along with Holland, had through its progressive liberalization of markets brought about capitalist development, had by the same token cultivated the competitive economy.[1] For differing reasons, the cultures that had accompanied this same development on the Continent were not only statist, but also favourable to co-operation among (national) firms rather than to mutual competition. In traditionally *dirigiste* France, and in Germany and Italy with their delayed development, State protectionism, publicly-owned firms, exclusive rights for public, and private, firms and consortia among private firms were common ingredients in the guidance of the

[1] cf. D. C. North and R. P. Thomas, *The Rise of the Western World* (Cambridge Univ. Press, Cambridge, 1973), and D. Landes, *The Unbound Prometheus* (Cambridge Univ. Press, Cambridge, 1969).

economy.[2] That a totalitarian regime like Italian fascism of the 1930s could go so far as providing for an obligatory consortium among all the firms in a sector when that met with the majority desire of the firms in that sector may seem incomprehensible to someone who has grown up in the culture of the Sherman Act. But in the European culture, it was merely an extreme form of a rooted principle, that the cartel was one of the positive manifestations of private associationism and of the freedom of trade: all the more positive if the cartel was operating with an eye to definite objectives of public interest and approved by public organs.[3]

## THE FREIBURGER ORDOLIBERALEN SCHOOL

Yet taking things to extremes sooner or later leads to extreme results, which cast doubt on the underlying principles and open the road to the sowing of opposite principles. The most pernicious extremism was what came in those same 1930s in Germany, where collaboration between the Nazi government and private cartels was one of the vehicles for the forced labour and then extermination of the Jews. It was on this lacerating, tragically pathological profile of a non-competitive economic system that a group of economists and lawyers began pondering in the German university of Freiburg. They highlighted, not dissimilarly from what had happened decades earlier in the USA, on the one hand the theme of non-legitimated private power; and on the other, the absolute need to give a solid institutional framework for the competitive economy

[2] D. Landes, *The Unbound Prometheus*, cited in note 1 above, p. 164 *et seq.*
[3] On the basis for cartels primarily in the German tradition, see M. Heidenhein and H. Schneider, *German Antitrust Law* (F. Knapp Verlag, Frankfurt, 1991) p. 17. The Italian Fascist law on consortia is Law No. 834 of 16 July 1932, superseded by Article 2616 of the 1942 Civil Code, which gave the government the power to set up obligatory consortia without even a request by those concerned (but this Article was never brought into effect).

to prevent both the formation of that power and the creation with it, by linking up with public power, of a conglomerate that could engender tragedies like the one Germany was then living through. What was to go down in history as the school of the Freiburger Ordoliberalen were also aware of the "excess" of public power that had to be restrained when it served to oppose private power, to which, accordingly, the constitutional framework in itself ought to furnish the antidotes. In short, with the most limpid clarity, the fundamental assumptions and consequent dilemma of antitrust law emerged.[4]

EARLY DEVELOPMENT OF ANTITRUST LAW

That first seed, which came without response and indeed in maximum secrecy, behind closed doors at a university, was destined to take root and yield its fruit in the period after the Second World War. But that rooting was not to be easy. Once the totalitarian regimes had been defeated, the principles of economic governance which they had, certainly, bent to their ends, but had not invented, retained much of their force. It was no coincidence that Germany was the first country on the Continent to adopt an antitrust law, in 1957. On the prevailing opinion, this was because of the stronger influence that the Americans then had in that country, but according to a more recent opinion was in fact through the role the Freiburg School played in postwar Germany. But the 1957 law was a compromise that showed marked differences from the initial bill presented

---

[4] The history of the School and its protagonists is told and their influence discussed by D. Gerber, "Constitutionalizing the Economy: German Neo-Liberalism, Comparative Law and the 'New' Europe" in (1994) 42 *The American Journal of Comparative Law*, 25. Gerber rightly notes that the obscurity it has fallen into is primarily due to the restricted spread of German in today's international academic community. But it had been discussed not so many years ago in A. Peacock and H. Willgerodt, *Germany's Social Market Economy* (Macmillan, London, 1989).

in the Bundestag by Franz Böhm, the Freiburg School's most illustrious lawyer, who had since become a member of parliament. One pillar of the Bill had been the creation of an independent antitrust authority, specifically to create a diaphragm between political and economic power and thus prevent them from colluding. The law set up the authority, but reserved for government the power of adopting decisions that might depart from its own, in the national interest. It concerned itself with preventing abuses of market power, but also left room for "crisis cartels", and directly exempted whole sectors from its prohibitions: banks, insurance, transport, and public utilities in general.

It is a fact, though, that other countries did not even have a law like the German one. Among these was Italy, where various bills had come before parliament from the early 1950s. One of them, written by the foremost Italian competition lawyer, Tullio Ascarelli, and presented by Ugo La Malfa and Riccardo Lombardi, was designed in surprising harmony with Franz Böhm's ideas. But nothing was done, even though parliamentary debates went on for more than two terms, and the theme was dropped in the early 1960s when a Commission of Parliamentary Inquiry into competition reached the conclusion that there were no worrying bottlenecks in Italy. That was not at all true, while it was instead the case that Italy was actually taking different pathways: it was responding to the bottlenecks there were, for instance in the oil or fertiliser markets, by throwing public enterprise into them with heavy competitiveness; and responding to the territorial lags in development by augmenting financial incentives and State aids, as well as by nationalizing the production and distribution of electric power and later allowing firms with State participation exclusivity in building and running infrastructures of industrial and civil utility. It was to take decisive impulse from the Community, in which the principles of competition had in the meantime been asserted, for Italy, among

# THE HERITAGE OF HISTORY 43

the last, to eventually adopt an antitrust law at the turn of the 1990s, in proximity with and in terms of completion of the single market, then scheduled for 1992.[5]

## ANTITRUST IN THE EUROPEAN COMMUNITY

Moreover, though less emphatically than in Italy, even at Community level the acceptance of the competitive economy had not been free of dispute. It is indeed true that competition appears in the very first articles of the Rome Treaty, among the fundamental principles, and that analytical provisions (Articles 85 *et seq*) are devoted to it, which prohibit first restrictive agreements and abuses of dominant positions of firms, secondly measures against competition itself by Member States, and finally the extension of exclusive rights beyond the "general interest" goals justifying them. But these norms, though in time to prove to be as it were magic boxes, capable of expanding their contents, were initially conceived in a much more limited context. On the one hand they were surrounded by other norms that stressed their subordinate value in relation to integration of the market (almost as if competition ought to be pursued no further than the limits of its serviceability for that end) and were, moreover, accompanied by the explicit assertion of the Treaty's neutrality in relation to the public or private ownership of firms; on the other, the climate in Member States—and the Community itself—was such as to bring competition up against a limit, sometimes explicit, sometimes implicit, in the industrial and agricultural

---

[5] Antitrust laws were adopted in France, Holland and Belgium more or less at the same time as the German law. Between 1970 and the early 1980s Luxembourg, Ireland, Greece and Portugal were added. Spain, which had already adopted a law before entering the Community while still under the Franco regime, adopted a new one more in line with the Treaty in 1990, and Ireland, Belgium and Portugal did the same shortly after. The United Kingdom and Denmark have remained in a different position on this point, with antitrust laws markedly divergent from the Community norm.

policies which, for public ends, used means incompatible with it. We were in fact for many years to have (and largely still do, indeed) a Common Agricultural Policy in which competitive principles have only very recently begun to operate; while there have been repeated industrial policy interventions, not just national but also at Community level, revolving around crisis "cartels", the allocation of production quotas to participating firms, and bans on imports at competitive prices.[6]

It would have been hard to emerge from this balance of ups and downs without the presence within the Commission of a strong pro-competition position, like the one gaining strength, with every institutional propriety, in DG IV, the Directorate to which guardianship of competition itself was entrusted. It would have been still less likely to happen had economic growth, the steady integration of the internal market and the gradual liberalization of the international one not by themselves asserted the rightness of that guardianship.

It should, however, be noted that within this evolution the subordination of competition to market integration showed that market integration could act not just as a limit but also (in the opposite direction) as a source of strengthened protection for competition itself. It was certainly a limit in the support it supplied to the Common Agricultural Policy and the above-described industrial policy measures, often justified by the safeguarding of common productive structures. But even before the tide began to turn, Community decisions in the antitrust area were already becoming more rigorous (by comparison with

---

[6] For an effective summary of the Common Agricultural Policy and its instruments see N. Nugent, *The Government and Politics of the European Union*, (Macmillan, London, 3rd ed, 1994). Ch. XIII. On crisis cartels in industry not just authorized but actually encouraged by the Community, see J. Bodoff, "Competition Policies of the U.S. and the EEC: an Overview" in (1984) E.C.L.R., 574.

American decisions on similar cases) towards the behaviour of firms segmenting the European market along national lines and thus acting against the primary goal of integration. The result, as we shall shortly see, was types of *per se* illegality that had never been seen in the USA.

The European antitrust history is, then, a necessarily and peculiarly European one, even if it did in the end reach, with the Maastricht Treaty, an assertion of competition as an autonomous fundamental principle, and the adoption of industrial policy at Community level which is understood no longer as a haven from competition but as a restructuring of the economy on competitive lines (and hence leading to the liberalization of sectors still covered by exclusive rights, and the implicit overcoming, perhaps, of the very neutrality between public and private ownership of firms that still remains embodied in the Treaty).[7] But to assess this history as a whole and understand what this final position really means, we have first to go over its individual parts and see how our peculiarities interacted with the basic principles and with the technical arguments whose development we have followed in American antitrust law.

[7] On this point see C. D. Ehlermann, "The Contribution of EC Competition Policy to the Single Market", in (1992) 29 *C.M.L.R.* 257. It should be added that a dissenting opinion saw the opposite principle in the new Article 130, namely, the requirements for Community neo-interventionism. A debate among several opinions on the point can be found in (1995) 1 *European Law J.* 23. The new Article 130 reads as follows: "the Community and the Member States shall ensure the conditions necessary for the competitiveness of the Community's industry", though without "introduction by the Community of any measures which could lead to the distortion of competition".

# 4. "RESTRICTIVE" AGREEMENTS

### THE NORMATIVE MACHINERY

The treatment of agreements comes about in Europe on the basis of normative machinery which, over and above the results it leads to, is clearly different from the American one. The provisions of the Sherman Act (and the laws that followed it) led to defining as restrictive those agreements that prove to be illegitimate, whether because they are "*per se*" restrictive, or because they are unreasonable and hence, today, devoid of an efficiency justification. That means that when there is a justification, the agreement is not regarded as restrictive (as occurred in common law, though on the basis of different criteria of reasonableness). Article 85(1) of the Treaty forbids all agreements, including concerted practices, which have "as their object or effect" the restriction of competition within the Common Market; it indicates in particular some types of prohibited agreements, from price-fixing to sharing of markets, discriminatory conditions, and control of access. However, Article 85(3) goes on to add that all the foregoing provisions may be declared inapplicable where the agreement contributes to improving production or promoting technical or economic progress and consumers have a fair share of the resulting benefit, as long as competition is not eliminated and there are no "restrictions which are not indispensable". In this case the Commission has the power to "exempt" the agreement from the application of Article 85(1), and may do so either by individual exemption or by general exemption, that is, indicating the categories of agreement (and possibly the relevant markets) that are *a priori* exempt, as long as they contain certain clauses and do not contain certain others, both analytically indicated in the exemption regulations.

This normative sequence has induced the Commission to interpret Article 85(1) very rigidly and to bring within the power of its exemption the same reasons as needed to regard a reasonable agreement as non-restrictive; with the result, generally but not always, that on the basis of Article 85(1) the only agreements cleared are where no restriction is contemplated in any way (apart from those quantitatively so insignificant as not to bring about appreciable effects on competition: a 1986 Commission communication sets at 5 per cent the market share for irrelevant agreements, provided always that the firms participating have a turnover below 300 million ECUs). A different interpretation would be possible (a point that is topical today, as we shall see below), but that might have given the exemption power the nature of a derogation, and hence an extension of the exemptions, more than has actually occurred; and this has led in application to the adoption of many of the lines of argument shaped around reasonableness and efficiency in the American courts. These are not the only ones, however, and alongside them we find on the one hand restrictive rigidities and on the other permissive flexibilities that are peculiarly European in origin.

## VERTICAL AGREEMENTS

This European duplicity, if we may so term it, is displayed in the first place in relation to vertical agreements. Our case law in this area has for long been (and largely still is) much more severe than the American case law after the turn in the *Sylvania* case, so much so that the presence of inter-brand competition is not always regarded as sufficient to justify (or at least render irrelevant) restrictions of intra-brand competition through agreements between producers and distributors or retailers. In the leading case in the area, *Consten & Grundig*, of 1966,[1] the Commission challenged the exclusive agreement for France that Grundig had given to Consten and had strengthened by barring its wholesale distributors in Germany and other countries from selling to France, where the price of Grundig products was kept higher than elsewhere, net of French tax. The parties maintained, first before the Commission itself and then before the Court of Justice, that Article 85 referred primarily to inter-brand competition, and that as far as intra-brand restrictions went, one had to presume efficiency in promoting inter-brand competition failing proof of the contrary. This argument copied word-for-word approaches of the Chicago School, which in fact at the time the American courts themselves had rejected, in the name of protection (dropped later in the *Sylvania* case) for the right of each distributor or retailer to exercise freedom of trade without restraint.

Our Court did not accept the arguments either, but for very different reasons. It accepted that inter-brand competition was the most relevant for the purposes of prohibition under Article 85, but added that this did not *a priori* exempt intra-brand restrictions, with the consequence—inconceivable today (and perhaps in earlier times too) for an American court—that the fact that the Commission was not concerned to ascertain the size of inter-brand competition was irrelevant. On this basis, the absolute territorial protection by which the exclusivity for France was guaranteed was illegitimate. It is indeed true, said the Court, that imports have an effect on the supply planning that Consten may engage in and on the organization of services it may offer customers. But a margin of risk is inherent in commercial activity, and in any case "the more manufac-

[1] *Consten and Grundig* v. *Commission* [1966] CMLR 418.

turers isolate themselves from each other in consumers' eyes, the more competition among them is reduced. Moreover, competition among wholesale distributors of products of one and the same brand enlivens the downstream market of sales to final consumers".

As we can see, these are very important assertions of principle that bring the decision close to the American ones of the 1960s. But there are two important differences, one explicit and the other implicit. The explicit one is that the need for intra-brand competition is based on protection not of an individual right (freedom of trade) but of a general and objective principle (competitiveness of the market in all its segments). The implicit one is that such a pervasive and rigorous principle is asserted to the extent that it serves to protect another principle, a higher one in 1966, that of market integration. For the territory protected by Consten's rigid exclusivity coincided with that of the French State, and both the Commission and the Court saw this protection as persistence of the segmentation of economic activities along national frontiers, violating the "Grundnorm" of the whole Community system.

We shall have to get used to the (less than excellent) habit of European case law of setting out heavy positions of principle (like this one on the value of intra-brand competition) that nonetheless have an underground relative value, with the consequence that they are later denied once the reason that led to their formulation is no longer at stake. It is certain that after *Consten & Grundig*, intra-brand restrictions were to be treated much more leniently when they did not raise the problem of segmentation along national lines; while the rigour of this first case was to remain when the same problem presented itself. Moreover, we shall soon find that the same absolute territorial protection, when it affects the relations between a small producer and a small distributor both seeking to enter a market, not only does not have "restrictive potential" but does not even "place European integration at risk" (this is the quantitative criterion formalized in the 1986 "*de minimis*" communication already mentioned). Only three years after the *Consten & Grundig* case, the Court exempted an exclusive relationship with absolute territorial protection between a German manufacturer with 0.1 per cent of the market and an equally small Belgian distributor.[2]

In *Pronuptia* v. *Schillgalis*,[3] the Court was for the first time called on to speak on franchising contracts. It did so without going into the facts, since it was in a context of a preliminary ruling, that is, merely supplying the national judge dealing with the case with the interpretation of Community law he has asked for pursuant to Article 177 of the EC Treaty. The question it was answering was whether the vertical restrictions inherent in the franchising relationship are compatible with Article 85, knowing that in this specific case the franchising generated exclusivity concerning not a whole Member State, but the Paris region only.

The Court accepted that the good functioning of franchising (the commercial utility of which it stressed) might require clauses protecting against competitors the knowhow the producer transfers to the retailer, making the retailer subject to requirements as to the location and decor of points of sale, and as to the selection of products to sell, and even publicity. If however the contract were to provide both for an obligation to sell only at the points of sale indicated by the manufacturer and for the retailer's right to absolute exclusiveness on a given territory, then, said the Court, this would entail a division of the market contrary to Article 85, as already decided in *Consten & Grundig* (though that, as the Court stressed recalling the *Völck* case, concerned an established brand, whereas it was quite possible that in order to venture on a new product a retailer

---

[2] *Volk* v. *Etablissements J. Veivaecke* [1969] CMLR 273.
[3] *Pronuptia de Paris GmbH* v. *Pronuptia de Paris Irnegard Schillgalis* [1986] CMLR 474.

might consider a solid exclusivity agreement necessary). Moreover, no restraint should be imposed on the seller's freedom of pricing.

*Pronuptia* is a problematic decision, opening a sort of transition. The Court well understood that if it accepted the efficiency of franchising it would perforce have to accept also the restrictive clauses it requires, including exclusive agreements with territorial protection. Moreover, in the specific underlying case (which it was not judging, but on which its decision would impinge) there was no national segmentation at stake. On the other hand, *Consten & Grundig* was there, and had set a general principle. The Court then on the one hand reaffirmed it, thus apparently from this viewpoint renewing its strength in still more expansive terms; on the other, however, it continued to circumscribe its scope to cases involving established brands, and let it be understood that territorial exclusivity, without absolute protection, might be allowed to pass.

Here came the transition. Two years later, in 1988, the Commission approved the exemption regulation for franchising that accepted territorial exclusivity as long as it was not accompanied by bans on parallel imports (the real theme of the *Consten & Grundig* case) but instead accompanied by the licensees' freedom to trade products among themselves.[4] Moreover, five years later, again giving a preliminary ruling in a case where a beer retailer, De Limitis, had undertaken to take supplies exclusively from Henninger, but was free to take these supplies in its own country or in other Member States, the Court expressed itself in terms now almost the same as the American ones following *Sylvania*.[5] It no longer made explicit reference to the need for intra-brand competition, and told the trial judge to verify carefully whether there was room for new entrants, bearing in mind that entry was harder in saturated

---
[4] Regulation No. 4087 of 1988.
[5] *Sergios De Limitis* v. *Henninger Brau A.G.* [1992] 5 CMLR 210.

markets in which, moreover, consumers were faithful to a limited number of big manufacturers. Attention was henceforth, as we see, entirely on inter-brand competition; it would seem to be the case that as long as it is there and in the absence of import bans, intra-brand restrictions are of much less interest.

There is, then, as in the USA, an evolutionary course. However, it is a different course, even though the outcome is similar. In Europe too the starting point was protection of intra-brand competition, but this was done, as we have noted, not in the name of individual freedom (the trader's), something always ignored with us, but to protect a principle, competitiveness in market integration, which with time would become increasingly less pressing and in any case generate a *per se* illegality, that of import restrictions. It was consequently not vertical agreements limiting intra-brand competition that were to be prohibited *per se* (except for price-fixing, which was never to be permitted even in this context), but only agreements containing that specific type of restriction.

This, it might be observed, is inter-state competition, and that is just what the European organs ought to be dealing with. That is a first possible conclusion. But it does not prevent us grasping the connotations of the underlying notion of competition and the relevant culture; or noting that, at least along the course highlighted thus far, we never glimpse the premises, and so the first doctrines, of American antitrust law. It is quite true the Court of Justice soon came round to accepting protection from the restrictions and abuses attacked by the Treaty not just in the Community bodies, but also before national judges themselves, because, it said, it was a matter of protecting rights the Treaty conferred on European citizens, which accordingly hold in every judicial instance. Yet perhaps because of its initial, and lasting, subservience to the principle of market integration, perhaps because of the persistence of a rooted culture of controlling the economy that was seeking its chance of continued existence, competition seemed itself to be not so much the content of individual freedoms as a principle of efficient organization, realization of which lent itself to being shaped in regulatory fashion in the context of the other principles that were to be protected in relation to the market. The result, as will emerge still better below, is that in Europe the balancing looks more like one between public purposes than the outcome of an encounter or clash between private freedoms.

That this is so is shown by the very existence of that European peculiarity of exemptions by category, along with the use made of them. The Commission, presumably in all sincerity, has always explained the institution not as a manifestation of a regulatory power but as a simplification and acceleration of decisions it was being called on to make in very numerous but all basically identical cases. Faced with this host of cases, argues the Commission, is it not better to say in general terms what clauses make particular types of contract compatible with competition or not, so as to avoid the loss of time in case-by-case litigation?

It is certainly better, and certainly that is what was meant to happen. Yet does there not remain a basic difference from checks through litigation if what are condemned or accepted are not restrictions associated with individual factual contexts, but contractual clauses in their abstract interpretation? It is quite true that the guidelines adopted from time to time by the United States Justice Department for identifying beforehand the cases on which to open inquiries and those instead to be treated as irrelevant are not much different. It is also true, on the other hand, both that the clauses accepted by the exemption regulations spring not from abstract deductions but from specific previous cases, and that the regulations themselves contain a final safeguard clause providing for non-exemption of the accepted clauses themselves in specific situations where, say, there is no inter-brand competition, and they therefore act so as to close the market.

Yet the existence of a sizeable number of exemption regulations covering industrial and commercial activities sometimes by sector (exclusive arrangements for car concessionaires) and sometimes transversely (franchising, specialization agreements, licensing or know-how agreements) may give renewed ground to an objectionable notion of competition presumed or not presumed on the basis of regulation (and on the basis of a weighting by public purposes extrinsic to protection of competition itself), rather than ascertained on the basis of the clash on the market between economic freedoms in their actual exercise. Which means that it is the hand of the sovereign, taking account of the interests at stake, that is tracing the boundary between antitrust power and freedom of enterprise, not constitutionally recognized solidity, in the field, of the specific freedoms of each and all.

### HORIZONTAL AGREEMENTS

Let us, though, confine ourselves for the present to these initial observations, and move on to deal with horizontal agreements. On an approach shared with the American case law, those with the object of fixing a common price between competitors and/or sharing out the market between them are those treated most severely, strengthened in Europe whenever those shares follow and isolate national markets; and a trend is emerging, at least in the Commission, towards a sort of *per se* invalidity of purely symptomatic practices going much further in its severity than the analytical verification of facts that at least in recent years has met with agreement by both scholars and judges in the USA.

In the *Dyestuffs* case, which dates back to 1969,[6] the

[6] The Commission's decision, which dates back to 1969, was confirmed by the Court of Justice in 1972 in *Dyestuffs* v. *Commission* [1972] CMLR 557.

Commission had noted a simultaneous price increase on the dyestuffs market, with equal differences in various national markets. The firms maintained that this was merely parallel behaviour, but the Commission felt it could discern evidence of concertation, first in the very fact of simultaneity, then in the similarity of the increases requested by various manufacturers, and finally in the repeated informal contacts among manufacturers themselves, allegedly with the specific object of prices.

Before the Court, the classic arguments from efficiency grounds were—not without technical basis—upheld to explain the parallel behaviour: it was said that the division of national markets through prices enabled the necessary technical assistance to be provided to users, and deliveries to be made immediately (since for small quantities they had to go through the national networks of agents). But for the Court the decisive thing was the fact that even when a direct relationship was set up between a manufacturer and a major user in another Member State, the price to the latter in general remained the one set beforehand for that State. That showed that the efficiency grounds, though valid, were not in fact determinant, and that the segmentation brought about "isolated users in their respective national markets, preventing general competition of manufacturers in the common market".

Over twenty years later, the Commission and the Court of First Instance were no less severe in a case where the presumed concertation, which in the case in point isolated and internally fragmented the British tractor market, resulted exclusively from intense, detailed exchange of information on sales by the manufacturers.[7] There were eight manufacturers; four of them covered 80 per cent of the British market, and with the system adopted each of them got to know each individual sale by each of the

---

[7] *John Deere Ltd* v. *Commission* [1994] ECR II-957.

others, and hence the respective position in each individual portion of the territory concerned. Both the Commission and the Court of First Instance agreed on maintaining that in such a concentrated market such high transparency among the (few) manufacturers was destroying the element of uncertainty that was essential in order for there to be any competition. The proof was among other things the situation the smaller manufacturers were put into: for them there was no advantage either in joining the information agreement (which would set quotas on their possible sales) or in staying out (since they would find it hard to sell even a single tractor). That showed that the agreement was in fact a device by the four biggest manufacturers to regulate and contain new entrants.

The conclusion in terms of principle was very drastic: the exchange of information was illegal, even if behind it there was no market-sharing agreement that it served to guarantee and implement. The restrictive agreement was consequently to be presumed as inherent in the agreement to share information. It would nonetheless be excessive to think that in a case of this type the severity displayed was born of extreme, nonchalant use of *"per se"* assumptions. The principle stated, read against the features of the case, seems strongly inspired by the facts, so much so as to suggest that even an American judge (today called on by the Justice Department to decide on parallel behaviour in oligopolistic markets) would reach the same conclusions, brought to them by the oligopolistic nature of the market, the weight in it of the very limited number (four) of big manufacturers, and the special analytic nature of the exchange of information, going well beyond the (more summary) data of usual information on the course of sales. Additionally, for the European judge, there was isolation of a national market.

The step towards more sharply presumptive use of symptomatic behaviour was taken by the Commission a little later in *Re Wood Pulp Cartel*.[8] Here it was faced with 40 manufacturers of wood pulp intended for paper manufacture, who supplied the European market through long-term contracts (up to five years), with the guarantee on the one hand of quarterly purchases of minimum quantities and on the other of prices no higher than they announced at the start of the quarter, though leaving each of them the capacity to negotiate higher quantities at prices that could even be lower. The quarterly announcements were notified to customers and agents and also published before the start of each quarter. The prices announced showed that Europe was divided into two zones, north and south, associated with the access points for the product, whereas in some contracts (though not in all) there were prohibitions on resale and on export.

The Commission, on the strength of the precedents that had so severely dealt with transparency in oligopolistic markets, attacked both the price announcements and their parallel courses as violations of Article 85(1), holding that each of these were symptomatic of agreements that did not require further elements of proof. The Commission's axe also fell on the resale and export bans. But this time the Court did not agree, and the "maxims" derivable from the precedents were not enough for it to ignore the specific facts of the case, marked on the one hand by very limited segmentation among national markets (the resale and export bans were in some contracts only) and on the other by two features typical of the wood pulp trade: the long-term contracts and the special rigidity of demand. Taking these two features into due account, said the Court, the fact that the announcements were simultaneous and public was primarily to be explained as a natural consequence of the long term of the contract (which brought transparency with it), while the price parallelism was in turn explicable

---

[8] *A. Ahlstroem Osakeyhitioe and others v. Commission* [1994] 4 C.M.L.R. 407.

in relation to the rigidity of demand. Accordingly, the Court deemed concertation not proved and annulled the Commission's decision, which was left standing only for the sections relating to the clauses barring resale and export.

The whole set of these decisions, more than any other line of cases, now shows clearly the degree to which the severity of European antitrust measures is associated with defence of integration of the Common Market. When integration is at stake, not just the Commission but also the Courts find behaviour restrictive on a quasi-presumptive ground. When instead integration is not at stake, the rigour of the quasi-presumptions is dropped and the Court, asking for analytical factual proof of the actual existence of the restriction, adopts the same standard of scrutiny as in American scholarly opinion and case law, which as we have seen has remained fairly high for agreements with the same object.

Where we once again depart from the transatlantic approach, this time in the opposite direction, namely towards less severity, is with agreements, again horizontal, that have joint industrial initiatives as their object. In the USA, efficiency grounds, which are now more or less assumed (failing proof to the contrary) in vertical agreements, have at least to be proved under the rule of reason in case of horizontal cartel arrangements, so that, as we have mentioned, even co-operative research might find obstacles when co-operation is extended to manufacture and distribution. This is not the case in Europe, where horizontal agreements of an industrial nature (going much further than innovative research) are given the path of exemption under Article 85(3), with the same ease as in the USA vertical agreements are declared non-restrictive when their opponents cannot find adequate arguments against their (assumed) efficiency.

The "VW–Ford" case is an exemplary one from this

viewpoint.[9] The two car manufacturers had decided to set up a new joint plant in a depressed area of Portugal (enabling them to benefit from regional incentives from public funds) to build a new model of "multipurpose van". In this segment of the car market (which the Commission, without being contradicted, regarded as an autonomous relevant market) several producers were competing with each other, among whom, however, Renault, with its "Espace", held a top position with a share of over 50 per cent. And it was none other than Renault, or rather Matra which as project designer shared the rights to the "Espace" with it, that opened fire against the planned joint venture, first before the Commission and then on appeal.

It was not disputed—and this had been the Commission's starting point—that according to the current interpretation of Article 85(1) the agreement was restrictive, given that two competing car firms were combining their manufacturing activities in the relevant market. What was doubted was the existence of the requirements for exemption on the basis of Article 85(3), which the Commission had recognized: were there really the improvements in production or the technological or economic progress required by that paragraph? If so, did consumers have a fair share of the resulting benefit? Was the agreement truly "indispensable" to the introduction of the new product to the market? Was there, finally, not a risk that the absence of competition in the limited context of the new manufacturing might generate a co-ordinating effect on other markets too, thus crossing the threshold of the allowed exemption?

---

[9] *Matra Hachette* v. *Commission* [1994] ECR II-595. The decision eloquently symbolizes the infiltrations of industrial policy that have long marked European antitrust law. It should however be said that in the USA too similar infiltrations came about in the 1980s to protect national industry, in the very same sector. See the "consent decree" accepting the joint venture between General Motors and Toyota (103 FTC 374, 1984).

In answering these questions, the Court concluded that:

(a) the improvement to production consisted in the fact that the new plant would be the first application of a manufacturing process recommended by authoritative research institutes (though the technique, known as "just in time", had for some time existed in Japan and was therefore not a novelty but an importation);

(b) the technical advance consisted in the putting together of techniques already in fact known, though never yet used together in the same process;

(c) the benefits to consumers existed because they were being offered a broader choice of models than in the existing situation, though these benefits could not be compared with the purely hypothetical ones of any possible competitive descent on the market by the two manufacturing firms, and any dynamics they might have had to show in order to compete;

(d) the agreement was indispensable because without it it would certainly not have been possible to achieve the project on the terms and in the place planned, that is, a particularly depressed area of Portugal, where it would allow the creation of a sizeable number of new jobs; and these "exceptional circumstances", while they would never individually have been enough to permit implementation of the project, had legitimately been assessed, together with others, by the Commission;

(e) the risk of co-ordination effects over and above the new manufacturing might actually be present in the project, but the Commission had, by imposing restrictions on exchanges of know-how and information as to its implementation alone, effectively ruled it out. This was especially so since the new vehicle, though jointly manufactured, would be marketed by the two firms with a partly different appearance, with their own brands and in competition with each other.

At the end of this sequence of arguments, there are two comments the reader may feel like making. The first is that the wrong complainant had made criticisms of the agreement that were more correct than the Court had held; considering a firm that at the time had by far the biggest share of the relevant market, an agreement that merely allowed two competitors to compete more aggressively with that firm does not appear particularly restrictive. At bottom the Court says this, and it may very well be the main reason for its decision. But the answers it gives to the individual objections are in several cases expressions of highly questionable antitrust canons.

In the first place, there is the ambiguous relevance/irrelevance allowed to the social profile of the affair: the expected jobs in a depressed area. It is an aspect that certainly interests the European Community, is in fact protected by specific instruments (from the Community regional policies to the review of State aids directed at similar ends), but does not fall within the antitrust purview, given that Article 85(3), analytical as it is, does not mention it among the grounds for exemption. In this case, however, it ended up having some weight; otherwise it would not have been mentioned, and certainly not to say it led to "exceptional circumstances", however additional.

Secondly, there are the very broad concepts both of productive improvement, and of technical progress, both detached from the proven presence of innovations that are the outcome of research and development and made instead to include in principle any organizational pattern capable of promising higher productivity. In these circumstances it amounts to an almost unbounded concept, applicable accordingly to the bulk of new manufacturing plants that replace previous installations. Thirdly, there is the basing of the benefit to consumers on the relationship with the existing position, and not instead with the one resulting from continuing competition between the two parties to the agreement. Under the apparent good sense of the arguments used (it is impossible to venture on hypothetical evaluations) there is, for a competition authority assessing the practices of firms in relation to their restrictive potential, a real error in law, explicable only by the specific features of the case: the complainant is the firm that (almost) dominates the market and will see a stronger competitor emerge from the agreement. If that is so, however, the argument ought to have been different, with the comparison involving on the one hand the competitive efficiency—against Matra-Renault—of the joint product, and on the other what separate products by VW and Ford might instead have led to.[10]

Over and above the substance of the decision, then, the principles of argument that result show surprising permeability of the antitrust principles, which are hybridized and weakened by the joint presence of industrial policy and social cohesion objectives. The original subsidiarity of the competition principle in relation to other principles laid down by the Treaty thus displays continuing vitality that goes well beyond the capacity for these principles to act as a merely external limit, going instead as far as corroding the sense and logic of the antitrust machinery from within.

What confirms this, moreover, is not just the horizontal agreements that in the past (though it would no longer be so today) the Commission approved, albeit outside the antitrust bodies and procedures, in order to overcome situations of industrial crisis, by authorizing and regulating production quotas per firm, minimum sales prices, import limits (which were, along with much of the Common Agricultural Policy, the most extreme examples of industrial policy as an external limit that compresses the antitrust

---

[10] Since antitrust law by definition gives priority protection to the potential positive effects of the dynamics of competition, these effects cannot be ignored as "hypothetical", but it should if anything be demonstrated that they are not reasonably foreseeable in the specific case.

space).[11] The confirmation comes above all from the Community antitrust scene itself and from the horizontal agreements which are still today exempted, not just individually like the one between VW and Ford, but also in general terms through appropriate regulations.

Suffice it to mention the general exemption for "specialization agreements", initially decided in 1972 and subsequently renewed and extended by further regulations in 1985 and 1993.[12] These recognized as legitimate agreements whereby several firms each concentrated on one or more products, or else undertook to manufacture others only jointly. Clearly this means that there will no longer be competition among the parties to the agreement on the products that each leaves up to the other, or that two (or more) decide to manufacture jointly. But the price of this absence of competition is, according to the exemption regulations, worth paying in the name of the more rational supply that results and the strengthening of the participating firms. It is true that exemption is not provided for indiscriminately, but only when the supply of products involved in the agreement does not exceed 20 per cent of the relevant market, and when the parties' total turnover does not exceed one thousand million ECUs annually. It is equally true, however, that the second limitation—a limitation to small and medium-size firms—was allowed to be derogated from by the last revision of the Regulation, in 1993, which also allowed firms with higher turnovers to notify their agreements to the Commission and be exempted if it did not oppose them within six months. And it is in any case true that the regulation reflects clear industrial policy thinking on the basis of which production rationalization, instead of being entrusted to market

---

[11] See above Ch. 3, text and note 6.
[12] The first regulation is No. 2779 of 1972. Those of 1985 and 1993 are Nos. 417 and 151 respectively.

selection, is organized through means aimed at favouring (primarily) smaller firms.

What is striking about Europe, as we have already said, is that this happens not just with machinery outside the antitrust area, but even internal to it. This is brought out further and very plainly by the most prominent cases of individual exemption of specialization agreements not covered by the general regulations. In 1983 ENI and Montedison, then among Europe's biggest firms in the chemical sector, divided up production and consequently became bound to each other, for the transition stage, by supply and processing agreements, thus complying with the Italian Government's "chemical plan" and seeking to remedy the structural over-capacity crisis that had hit the sector throughout Europe. Yet in 1987 the Commission gave a positive answer to an individual exemption request, though finding not just "elimination of the previously existing competition between the two firms", but also the impact on their possible future competition of the collaboration necessary in order to implement the specialization agreement. Nonetheless, the exemption was justified by the benefit of production rationalization in a situation of over-capacity, by the greater ease of rationalization if secured through agreement, and by the fact that the free play of competition would not have allowed restructuring as rapid or also as "comprehensive" and "incisive".[13]

It is very unlikely that a decision like this would be taken today, after the long evolutionary process that has led to industrial policy as promotion of competitive markets, instead of subordinating antitrust to industrial policy. The fact remains that before this decisive final transition, considerations like those just referred to were part of the antitrust baggage, though more proper to the language of industrial policy than to that of "business defence" against antitrust agencies; or at most halfway between them.

[13] Eni/Montedison, case IV/31.055, in OJ L 5/13,1987.

# 5. ABUSE OF A DOMINANT POSITION

### "SPECIAL RESPONSIBILITY"

Abuse of a dominant position, though taking the shape of conduct at least in part corresponding to what the analytical indications in the American Clayton Act are aimed at, is a peculiarly European creature.[1] It is so, in the first place, conceptually: the EC Treaty does not provide in any case for dismantling a firm that has grown so much as to shelter itself from even potential competition (nor, moreover did its provisions even include the ban on merger and concentration contracts to enable that point to be reached: they were to be barred only later in the 1989 Regulation (No. 4064) on mergers). In the absence of the sanction of divestiture which by contrast accompanies the American provisions mentioned, the dominant position is accepted in principle, at least (after entry into force of the regulation on mergers) when reached through competitive growth and not by putting several firms together. This means, then, that having market power is not in itself against the

---

[1] Our "abuses" are however more numerous than the restrictive practices indicated by the Clayton Act (see above, Ch. 1 under "Prohibitions to protect market pluralism increase"), which have, moreover, over time been almost entirely brought under the "rule of reason" laid down by the Chicago School. Over and above that is the historical rootedness in Europe of acceptance of a dominant position, and repression of its abuse only. Not everyone recalls that the Weimar Republic had already adopted a law in 1923 "against abuses of dominant positions" (on this see, recently, F. M. Scherer, *Competition Policies for an Integrated World Economy* (The Brookings Institution, Washington DC, 1994) p. 26).

competition rules. But those who acquire it and are therefore in a dominant position are from that point on seen as having a "special responsibility" barring them from behaviour allowed their competitors on the same market, to the extent that there are any left.[2] Market power, just because it is conceptually accepted, is thus loaded with the burdens and limits which, according to the general principles more of public than of private law, bear upon whoever holds power. One outcome is singularly divergent from the USA: there that power, once it gets beyond certain limits, meets (at least in theory) the sanction of last resort, dismantling, but until then, as long as the market is not completely closed, acts of "aggressive" competition by its holder are as lawful as anyone else's; here the firm can never be broken up, but the special responsibility of those holding power subjects them to antitrust measures in some cases more severe than they would meet with in the USA, or those a normal competitor meets with in Europe too.

In the specific cases, this is reflected in ambiguously broad statements of principle in relation to the type of practices prohibited, in particularly rigid use of some of the common concepts: abuse, discriminatory practices, and practices aimed at exclusion, and in frankly regulatory handling of the type of abuse already most differing in the EC Treaty provisions from the American antitrust tradition, the practice of "excessive" prices.

[2] "Independently of the reasons why it has such a dominant position, an enterprise possessing it has the special responsibility not to allow its own behaviour to endanger genuine, undistorted competition in the Common Market". So the European Court in *Michelin* v. *Commission* [1985] 1 CMLR 282. The special responsibility which, as we shall see, is protection of weak competitors, was explicitly expanded by the Commission itself on the basis of the principle of "fairness". See V. Korah, *EC Competition Law and Practice* (London, 1994) p. 67, and L. Gyschen, *Abuse of Monopoly Power* (1988 Fordham Corporate Law Institute (B. Hawks ed.) 1989), p. 615. It may be useful to add that among the novelties introduced in 1980 into German competition law was the "relatively dominant position", a source of possible abuses by a firm that only "relatively" dominates small and medium-sized enterprises.

## ASSESSMENT OF "DOMINANT POSITION"

But let us first consider the premises for all this, namely the assessment of the dominant position. It is arrived at after a survey, very often disputed between the Commission and the firm, of the "relevant" market both from the product market viewpoint (the more products substitutable with each other, the broader is the market; the fewer the substitutable products, the narrower is the market) and in geographical terms (where there is a similar correlation, this time in spatial terms). On this basis, on the recurrent definition in the European case law, a firm is in a dominant position when it can act independently of the other producers or distributors (of the same good or service and substitutable goods or services); which means that the latter are crippled competitors, since their presence or behaviour is not capable of affecting the choices of the dominant firm, which keeps its prices unchanged even if they cut theirs, or else still maintains its market share whatever their efforts to erode it.

The definition—apparently clear in being tied to the "independence" of behaviour—in fact has two related aspects that make it ultimately highly problematic. The first concerns the correct recognition of the market position it applies to (with all its consequences); the second concerns the difference between this situation and that of the monopolistic market. The dominant position is not recognized on the basis of a single, unambiguous element of identity. According to the consistent European case law, market share certainly has great weight, but is rarely enough on its own; the higher the share is—say 80 per cent—the more likely it is that the firm that has it will be found to be in a dominant position. But that will not necessarily happen if that share is not stable, if there are no legal or economic "barriers" to the entry and/or expansion of competitors, and if these are proving capable of increasing their respective shares.

Conversely, it is possible for a firm to be found in a dominant position even with a much lower share, even under 50 per cent, if this share is much higher than its competitors, and if these are not able to grow; not necessarily because this is impossible, but because it is made particularly hard by, say, the size of the investments needed or the length of time taken to establish a new name on a market where brand loyalty counts (in the *Michelin* case, one of the grounds of Michelin's dominant position was in the fact that for the main customers, namely transport firms, expenditure on tyres is very high, which makes them very reluctant to change brand). What can be deduced from these features? That the dominant position is seen in situations other than monopolistic ones, where competition has not disappeared but has weakened, entry barriers are not necessarily prohibitive but are troublesome enough, and in short the market is not closed, though near it, making it likely it soon will be. These are accordingly unclear situations, in most cases ascertained with wide room for evaluation, based both on assessment of what has happened and on probabilistic estimates of likely future scenarios. What is the consequence? That what used to be market freedom is, on the basis of this sort of evaluation, dubbed market power, but a power that is not uprooted but merely contained in its manifestations. The resulting answer to the crucial antitrust dilemma thus once again displays a peculiarly hybrid nature, where regulatory tradition and the culture of competition meet and blend: the formation of private power is opposed in Europe very often at the stage before antitrust intervention would be legitimate in the USA, not just according to the most extreme followers of the Chicago School but also according to those who fear the consolidation of that power more than the obstructive interventions of public power. Moreover, the analysis itself by which market power is assessed in the two systems is, at least partially, different. As we will see below, the enforcement of the 1989 Merger Regulation is now reducing the gap, but for a long time in assessing dominant positions Europeans were ready to recognize symptoms of market power in markets the structure of which would have implied the absence of it for American analysts. Finally, action against market power, while on the one hand it does not and cannot go so far as divestiture, on the other comes down to prescriptions and proscriptions as to practices, which, as we shall see, tend to be more penetrating than those that anyone would, still, impose in the USA (on antitrust bases), therefore taking on a frankly regulatory connotation: between the channelling of market freedom and the prevention of market power, there is an intermediate band in Europe, namely protection of weak competition against the strongest competitors.

### ABUSE AS AN "OBJECTIVE CONCEPT"

In the USA abuse is brought under attempts at monopolization and is accordingly distinct both from competitive acts, however aggressive, and from practices that are a natural consequence of technological or organizational improvements that have legitimately permitted growth on the market. It must, accordingly, have to do with conduct planned and pursued to the end of excluding others from the market or preventing them from gaining access to it, with the effect of reducing consumers' welfare.[3] One clarification should immediately be made in this connection, to avoid one discussion that often comes up, of a difference that in fact does not exist between the USA and Europe. It is not true that in the USA the forbidden conduct of the

---

[3] An exemplary and explicit case here is *Aspen Skiing Co.* v. *Aspen Highlands Skiing Corp.* 472 US 585 (1985): with the important clarification, made by the Supreme Court in *Spectrum Sport* v. *McQuillan* 113 S.Ct. 884 (1993), that one also has to show the "dangerous likelihood of the securing of monopoly power".

holder of market power has to be "anomalous", and thus outside the type of practices allowed by contrast on a competitive market, where in Europe (only) we would reach the point of barring the firm in the dominant position from conduct allowed a normal competitor.[4] This non-existent difference in fact arises not from a comparison of the two case laws but from the conceptual uncertainty to be found on the European side, which in its most authoritative and most cited precedent, the *Hoffmann-La Roche* case,[5] had seen as abuse the mere "recourse to different methods from those arising in normal competition", while in more recent decisions it has explicitly been held that even practices normally allowed may not be when the effect is further to weaken already fragile competition with the firm employing them.[6]

In fact, though within to some extent different limits and premises, the position is the same in both the USA and in Europe, so that it is not here that the European distinctiveness is to be found. It is true that both in the USA and in Europe the holder of market power may be barred from "anomalous" conduct, for instance the practice of predatory prices, or from conduct "normal" in type, for instance exclusive distribution or refusal of supply. Where does the difference arise? In the different standards of assessment on one side or the other, in the USA leading to illegality only when both the effect of exclusion and of reduction of consumer welfare appear together, while in Europe they are oriented to the special responsibility of firms in dominant positions to protect existing small competitors and hence in any case take account of possible damage to such competi-

[4] So P. Jebsen and R. Stevens, "Assumptions, Goals, and Dominant Undertakings: the Regulation of Competition under Article 86 of the European Union" in (1996) 64 *Antitrust L.J.*, 443.

[5] *Hoffmann-La Roche* v. *Commission* [1979] 3 CMLR 211.

[6] So the Court of First Instance in *BPB Industries Ltd. & British Gypsum Ltd.* v. *Commission* [1993] 5 CMLR 32, and in *TetraPak Int'l* v. *Commission* [1995] ECR II-762.

tors, identifying it as abuse. And abuse, as the Court by no means coincidentally said in *Hoffmann-La Roche*, is an "objective" concept, which may thus even ignore the intentions of whoever commits it.

Let us then look at the similarities and differences relating to individual types of abuse that arise from these premises. Predatory pricing is forbidden in both the USA and Europe. In the USA, at least on the basis of the most recent case law, to secure the prohibition it must be shown not just that the prices are below cost, but also that those applying them have a reasonable prospect of more than recovering the investment in predation. Only if there is such prospect is there an abuse, since it proves that the selling at a loss will result in eventual and net consumer harm. If instead the loss is not recoverable on a market where, despite the elimination of competitors, consumers get only the benefit of the low price, then the case is one not of abuse but of aggressive competition, which is not forbidden.[7]

This is not the way things are in Europe. About the same time, in 1991, the Court of Justice dealt with the *Akzo* case,[8] in which not just prices below variable costs but also those below average total costs (though above the average of variable costs) were declared abusive on the basis of the sole consideration that the object was to eliminate a competitor. In Europe, moreover, we have sizeable case law regarding discounts to distributors and/or retailers, and the now-established principle is that a firm in a dominant position is allowed only transparent discounts associated with sales volume; not those given some and not all, ignoring sales volume, still less those conditional on refusing to sell competitors' products.[9] There is no comparable American

[7] *Brooke Group Ltd. v. Brown & Williamson Tobacco Co.* 113 S.Ct. 2578 (1993).
[8] *AKZO Chemie BV v. Commission* [1993] 5 CMLR 215.
[9] The principle has been firm since *Hoffmann-La Roche*, cited in note 5 above.

case law (though this is itself an indication). One may nonetheless ask whether in the USA a case like *British Gypsum* would be decided the same way: the additional discount offered only to resellers buying exclusively was found actually to have the purpose of allowing promotional and publicity investments. The Commission and the Court of First Instance did not give weight to this circumstance, and regarded the discount as an abuse.[10] If in so doing they were applying the principle of the "objective" nature of the abuse, they were certainly on a different path from the one an American court would follow. Had it instead in the same case been shown that the discount was one of the means used by the firm in dominant position to increase the costs of existing and potential competitors, it is quite possible by contrast that the divergence would be more apparent than real.

### INDIVIDUAL TYPES OF ABUSE

Another classical and frequent case of abuse in Europe is that of a firm in a dominant position on one market expanding into another. At this point, the conduct it pursues on the second market is subject to the same close scrutiny of abuse whenever there is "contiguity" between the two, thanks to which its dominant position on the first gives it an advantage on the second too. This is very clear in the case of a firm that is the monopolist of a network and starts competing with others to offer services on the same network. In this case, however, the "refusal to deal" comes in, which is not permitted to those controlling an "essential facility" with the symmetrical obligation of not applying discriminatory conditions on it.[11] An almost equally

---

[10] This case was cited in note 6 above.

[11] The "essential facility" doctrine was imported into Europe from the USA, where it was accepted in most explicit terms in *MCI Communication Corp. v. AT&T Co.* 708 F. 2d 1081 (1983), on the basis (according to some) of

clear case is that of a firm in a dominant position in production of a raw material entering manufacture of goods produced using it.[12] Less clear by contrast is the case of a dominant position being extended not vertically but horizontally from one product to another; and the case in which these differing characteristics are mixed.

TetraPak was a firm in an absolutely dominant position on the market for aseptic packaging (and the machines to make them). It decided to enter the different market of non-aseptic packaging, adopted contracts tying products on the two markets together and began to apply low-cost prices on the neighbouring market for non-aseptic packaging. Both practices were condemned as "abuses" even though they were on a market where Tetrapak did not have a dominant position.[13] Would American courts have done the same? In 1980 the Supreme Court denied *certiorari* against a decision of a Federal Court, according to which a firm was not violating section 2 of the Sherman Act when one of its branches had a monopoly of the market on which it was operating and this benefited another on its market, since it was to be considered that this competitive advantage was the outcome of efficient organization and superior ability in developing complementary products and reducing transaction costs.[14] Here again the difference might be seen as lying in the European "objective" notion of abuse, which can punish "superiority"

the remote precedent of the Supreme Court in *United States* v. *Terminal Railroad Ass'n* 224 US 383 (1912).

[12] *Istituto Chemioterapico Italiano and Commercial Solvents* v. *Commission* [1974] 1 CMLR 309.

[13] This is the *TetraPak* II case, already cited in note 6 above. It should however be noted that the Court of Justice, recently confirming the Court of First Instance's decision, specified that only "exceptional circumstances" can justify extension of Article 86 to a contiguous, non-dominated market. See *TetraPak International* v. *Commission*, 1996 ECR I–5951.

[14] As a consequence of the Supreme Court's denial of *certiorari* the Appeal Court decision was confirmed: *Berky Photo Inc.* v. *Eastman Kodak Co.* 444 US 1093 (1980).

when it is a threat to existing competition (even though this is not necessarily already weakened on the neighbouring market).

"Excessive" pricing is, as already mentioned, the type of abuse that perhaps says most about the European treatment of the firm in a dominant position and the notion of "special responsibility" that is its inspiration. Excessive price to whom, and protecting what? Seen as a breach of competition, it ought to be an abuse if and insofar as it damages competition itself, which can actually happen whenever an enterprise in a dominant (or monopoly) position in ownership of networks or production of raw materials also produces services that use the network or goods that need those raw materials, in competition with others. In this case there is abuse if by practising high prices not linked to cost it damages its competitors on the downstream markets, consequently strengthening itself. In this framework, the case looks like a sub-species of discriminatory practices and thus comes under typical antitrust evaluative canons. It is quite true that in the presence of network services disciplined as public services one might expect the specific regulatory authorities, not the antitrust ones, to lay down or at least assess the non-discriminatoriness of the interconnection and access charges required from suppliers of competing services. But when there are no regulatory authorities, and in any case in markets that do not fall under any special discipline, it naturally falls within the antitrust purview to assess whether charges of this sort have efficiency grounds or are a means of "raising rivals' costs", in a formula typical, as we saw earlier, of the most recent American approaches.

The fact is that in Europe, on the basis of a by no means forced reading of Article 86 of the EC Treaty, an excessive price is taken to mean not just one applied to competitors in the situations described, but also directly to consumers where the firm has a (legal) monopoly or is in a dominant position. In these terms, even accepting that the problem exists (and it may very well) it is not a problem of protecting competition. It is not, by definition, in the case of a firm with a legal monopoly; still less in the case of a firm in a *de facto* monopoly or a dominant position. For one of two things must hold: either there are actual or potential competitors for whom the "excessive" price to the detriment of consumers in fact constitutes the classical room for facilitating entry (it would not make sense, otherwise to prohibit as an abuse a firm in a dominant position selling below cost in order to eliminate that space); or there are no competitors, in which case the policy of excessive prices without market response leaves as the only means of protecting competition the break-up of the *de facto* monopoly or dominant position.

Europe does not provide for this. It starts from acceptance in principle of a dominant position, and at that point extends protection of competition to the protection of consumers who do not have it (or not much of it, which is a further complication), so as to put them artificially in a position as similar as possible to that of a competitive market. But this is no longer antitrust law; it is straightforward regulation of a firm in a dominant position.

The case law that has been taking shape on this aspect of "excessive price", moreover, confirms this. The best known case is the one when the French copyright-collection society was condemned because its charges to discothèques and dance halls (where it collects the rights on the music played) were found "excessive" since they were far higher than the averages in other European countries.[15] Other partly similar cases were *General Motors* and *British Leyland*,[16] in which each of these car manufacturers, enjoying (like all of them) the legal monopoly over the

---

[15] *Ministère Public* v. *Tournier* [1991] 4 CLMR 248.
[16] *General Motors Continental* v. *Commission* [1976] 1 CMLR 95. *British Leyland Ltd.* v. *Commission* [1986] ECR 3263.

issue of the approval certificates needed for the vehicles to be allowed on the roads, charged for them in the case of imported cars to a degree that was found excessive. In both cases there was careful verification of the relationship between prices charged and costs incurred for the service, and in both cases the costs did not justify the prices. It should however be said that the Court found decisive the fact that this was really aimed at discouraging parallel imports (and hence sales, even of their own cars, though in competition on the geographical market of manufacture).

## IN CONCLUSION

In conclusion, perhaps nothing can be more symptomatic of the factors that come together in European antitrust culture than this survey, albeit rapid, of abuse of a dominant position. In considering abuse the old and the new come together and in doing so become equally topical: the new thing is competition, the idea that private power is simply a degeneration of freedom against which the freedoms of all must be guaranteed; the old one is the supremacy of State power, which allows it to set itself above not just the freedom but also the powers of private individuals, indeed making it the most suitable instrument to confront such powers while tolerating their existence and controlling their excesses. These are two antithetical principles which our history has brought together and our antitrust provisions have found within themselves, with the ambivalent results we have been seeing.

It may be said that the USA too accepts private power, indeed to the point of not even setting those hybrid restraints on it that we do; and in their greater tolerance towards it, they solve the problem by refusing to call it power, continuing to see it as a natural manifestation or expression of private freedoms, and for this very reasons preferring it to the intrusions of public power. This is absolutely true, but our comparison has not been made in order to award either side the palm of victory, but only to understand. In this area we can only say, to each his own.

# 6. PROHIBITIONS OF DOMINANT POSITION

### MERGERS: THE BAN AND ITS LIMITS

Concentrations among firms are, as we know, disciplined not through the EC Treaty but by a Council Regulation (No. 4064), which came in 1989 after an extremely long gestation, starting in the early 1970s when mergers leading to total foreclosure of the market began to be treated as abuses of a dominant position.[1] This initial solution soon proved inadequate, if only because it assumed that one of the firms engaged in the merger was already in a dominant position. If instead two firms joined together that were strong but not to that point, and by joining together were left without competitors, there was no obvious remedy.

One might perhaps ask why the remedy was sought, if it is true as it was that the initial European antitrust approach was not hostile to a dominant position but only to its abuse, so much so, as we have repeatedly stressed, that it did not provide for divestiture. The reasons ought however already to be clear. One is the difference between natural growth and growth by contractual aggregation: these lend themselves to different treatment. The other, not immediately obvious to the non-expert, already emerged in relation to abuses: drawing a difference between a dominant position whose abuses are struck down, and one liable to be prohibited on the basis of the merger regulation. They are not the same thing; they are clearly in sequence, since the first has

[1] *Continental Can* v. *Commission* [1973] CMLR 199.

competition, however weak, that might regain force, where the latter, in order to be prohibited, must not have any at all any more, or not be likely to have any in the reasonably foreseeable future (a point already present even in the *Continental Can* case: a company already in a dominant position was regarded as abusing it by purchasing a competing firm, thus reaching the foreclosure of the market that years later was to be prohibited by Regulation No. 4064). The difference is thus not, as has been written,[2] due to a different attitude by the Commission, as being more reluctant to prohibit mergers since here the sanction is to make them void (thus a form of break-up, but only in relation to the future), while in the case of abuse what is attacked is only a practice, so that it is less attentive to defining a firm's position as "dominant". The reason for the difference goes much deeper. It goes to the basic features and hence peculiar hybridizations of European antitrust law containing both regulation, in order to preserve competition, of strong but not necessarily exclusive positions, defined as dominant within the meaning of Article 86 of the EC Treaty, and the 1989 prohibition on exclusive positions (only) if reached through purchase or merger.

If any importance is to be attached to the Commission's attitude towards the difference, it can and must be related to the more analytical investigations it undertakes in cases of merger, where there is not that "impressionistic" flavour that could be perceived in its analysis of markets, the state of competition and the size of entry barriers in so many cases of abuse. The same courses are now being taken with methodological rigour and factual scruples that are increasingly close to those of the most recent American case law. But this change has come with the times, with increased familiarity with that case law and the underlying theories, so that most recently the same features have begun to be

[2] I. Van Bael and J. Bellis, *Competition Law of the European Community*, 3rd edn. (CCH Europe, 1994) p. 434.

extended even to dealing with cases of abuse (where the dominant position is over "weakened" competition, not excluded competition).

There is a final element to take into consideration as regards mergers, namely the possibility, considered in the Regulation itself, that after the first challenge there may be actual negotiations between the parties and the Commission, on the conditions compliance with which would lessen the market power of the nascent firm, so as to free it from the prohibition (not taking one part in the case of take-over, or commitment to sell part to third parties in cases of merger). This happens frequently: the Commission finds greater room for assessment here, and in every case, to the extent that it decides that and on what terms the merger will be allowed, it further restricts the space for the dominant (merged) positions that are prohibited.

In this context, which seems to be shifting our own antitrust position towards the highly reductive boundary at which the more orthodox followers of the Chicago School in the USA take their stance—namely the boundary of total market foreclosure that allows restriction of output—it may seem contradictory for the Commission to make the kind of assessment that is done of grounds of enterprise efficiency. There is indeed in the case law on mergers a vein of severity that makes efficiency an additional danger point, liable to give still further distance from possible competitors and to act as a barrier to entry. This is very far not just from the positive evaluation generally given to efficiency in the USA, but also from what happens in Europe in relation to agreements, where there is even greater generosity in seeing "productive improvements" and "technical progress", able as such to provide exemption for plainly restrictive agreements. This contrast is striking and has been criticized.[3] The explanation given

[3] On this point see A. Jacquemin, "Horizontal Concentration and European Merger Policy" in (1990) 34 European Economic Review, 539, and

attributes it to the wording of the Regulation, since it indicates technical and production improvements among factors to be borne in mind in the judgment, but specifying that they must go to benefit consumers and not "obstruct" competition; they accordingly do not, it has been said, have any force for exemption. In fact any more than superficial analysis of the European case law brings out a less simplistic picture. On the one hand, over and above the growing methodological similarities (which can be approved), European case law has not gone so far as the reductive principles of Chicago, since it sees reasons for prohibition in the presence of obstacles to entry that Chicago would not always elevate to the rank of entry barriers. On the other hand it is true that efficiency grounds do not prevail over the obstacles the merger erects against competition, but they do not prevail only when those obstacles amount to total foreclosure (even if ascertained using a non-restrictive concept of entry barrier).

What then are in practice the situations in which market foreclosure has or has not been seen following a merger? Mention should be made, in order once more to stress the difference between this foreclosure and (already) dominant positions, of the *TetraPak-Alfa-Laval* case, 1991,[4] in which TetraPak, the main manufacturer of machines for aseptic packaging in cardboard containers, joined up with Alfa-Laval, one of the main producers of machines for aseptic processing, in particular of milk. The Commission found that TetraPak had a dominant position on its side, namely the packaging machines, where it had one "effective" competitor entirely incapable in the short to medium term of increasing its market share. To this (already) dominant position, said the Commission, the merger with Alfa-Laval added nothing, since to customers the bundled offer of

F. Jenny, *EEC Merger Control: Economics as an Antitrust Defence or an Antitrust Attack?* (1992 Fordham Corp. Law Inst. (B. Hawks ed.), 1993 p. 591).

[4] *TetraPak Rausing S.A. v. Commission* [1991] 4 CMLR 334.

both types of machines (for packaging and for processing) was not so important as to make separate purchase not preferable whenever Alfa-Laval's competitors, which exist, offered processing machines more advantageously.

Here it is not the conclusion of the case as such that is of interest, but the starting point: a position of TetraPak, already dominant, was nonetheless accompanied by one "effective" competitor, and could tolerate further additions before becoming reclusive and hence liable to prohibition. It should be recalled that because of the same position TetraPak was condemned shortly after for the abuses referred to in the foregoing pages.

It is significant that in relation to mergers the tolerable market shares reach high levels, up to the limits of almost totality, when there is, without coming up against barriers, potential competition. In *Alcatel-Telettra*,[5] the two companies, both manufacturers of telephone equipment, together covered over 80 per cent of the Spanish market, represented by the demand from the monopoly company Telefónica. But the merger was not prohibited, because Telefónica had a diversified policy and would accordingly after the merger certainly approach competing firms, which existed and were very strong (from AT&T to Siemens) and ready to come in. In *Mannesmann-Hoesch*,[6] the firm resulting from the merger would have had 90 per cent of the German market for gas pipe, and initially would certainly be safe from any effective competition. But because of the imminent, already scheduled, entry into force of the Community Directive opening tenders to any competitor in Europe, the barrier protecting that 90 per cent would disappear and other strong firms, like Ilva and British Steel, could attack it. Very similarly (perhaps even more obviously) in *Mannesmann-Vallomer-Ilva*,[7] a merger

[5] *Alcatel/Telettra*, case No. IV/M.042, 1991.
[6] *Mannesmann Hoesch*, case No. IV/M.222, 1992.
[7] *Mannesmann/Vallomer/Ilva*, case No. IV/M.315, 1994.

was allowed that brought together three of the strongest manufacturers of seamless steel pipe despite the risk of "interdependence" with the only significant remaining competitor in Europe. The reason was that "there is a specific threat on the market of competition" from Japanese manufacturers, not present at the moment but ready to undermine any "parallel anti-competitive behaviour" (though it should not escape us that here the potential competition is undoubtedly even more just a possibility, while on the other side the closure of the European market would come not directly from the merger but only from the high probability of consequent collusion between the last two remaining manufacturers).

If these are the criteria, on the one hand the forbidden merger will be one where competition is manifestly being eliminated, while on the other in most cases there will be broad room for negotiation to avert the disputed merger reaching that point. The best known prohibited merger was in fact between Aérospatiale and Alenia, manufacturers of the ATR 42 turboprop crafts, and De Havilland, a Canadian division of Boeing manufacturing the Dash 8, the strongest competitors on the same markets.[8] The Commission arrived at the prohibition taking account specifically of the disappearance of De Havilland as a competitor, the weakness of the other (few) manufacturers in the field, the absence of synergies between jet manufacture and turboprop manufacture (which ruled out entry by the big jet manufacturers), the non-existence of other potential competitors (there were a few companies in Eastern Europe, which would however have manufactured for Eastern Europe) and of the difficulty in any case of entering the market, given the whole set of investments each customer has to make when buying planes (staff training, repairs and maintenance). In this overall position the very

---

[8] *Aerospatiale/Alenia/De Havilland*, case No. IV/M.053, 1991.

efficiency of the merger—the nascent firm would have been the only one able to supply the whole range of turboprop aircraft, from smallest to biggest—helped to take the firm itself away from any competition whatever, making it able quickly to reach monopoly, and raise prices at its whim.

At first glance, the *Nestlè-Perrier* case had strong elements of resemblance with the one just considered.[9] Two of the three biggest producers of mineral water sold in France were to merge, in a situation where it had been shown (from the differing price trends) that all the local mineral waters were unable to compete with the national ones, purchasers were very fragmented and hence had no balancing contractual power, imports could not be counted on and there was no room for the entry of new manufacturers exploiting French water. Again on first consideration, the case left open only one dilemma, connected with a planned sale of springs from Perrier to BSN, the third big firm remaining in the market: had the sale not been made, Nestlè-Perrier's dominant position would have been unchallenged. If the sale had come about, then according to the Commission the market would have taken a duopolistic shape, leading to inevitable joint dominance by Nestlè-Perrier and BSN, on the basis of which it would equally have prohibited the merger. There was some boldness in the second assumption, if only because it has been found questionable that Regulation No. 4064 allows joint control to be challenged.[10] But there are two points of

---

[9] *Nestlè/Perrier*, case No. IV/M.190, 1992.

[10] In paragraphs 110 to 116 of the decision, the Commission puts forward considerable effort of argument to show that joint dominance, though not explicitly provided for by the Regulation, ought nonetheless to be included because that restriction of competition which is prohibited when it is the result of an individual dominant position cannot be allowed when it results from the domination of several firms. It is a fact, though, that the Court, only two years later in 1994, was to accept joint dominance only in relation to Article 86 and only in the presence of formal legal links among several enterprises

interest here: the first is that in order to make the prohibition the Commission was foreseeing a position of total non-competition, for lack of both current and potential competitors. The second is that following the challenges Nestlè and Perrier offered mitigating conditions it accepted, which led to a green light for the merger: on the one hand the sale to BSN would be improved, on the other, springs and licenses for manufacturing capacity able to render a new entrant competitive would be sold to a third party, to be identified by agreement with the Commission itself. That would take the market out of duopoly, which the Commission saw as inevitably collusive; and lead to a market structure similar to the one before the merger. There was, however, a great deal of hypothesizing in all this, but once the prohibition had been set at the boundary of total market closure, it was consistent to prevent that boundary being reached, through new commitments by the parties.

For this very reason, one of the few other merger prohibitions, probably motivated by specific grounds, seems out of step with these decisions. In 1995, RTL, Veronica and Endemol were combining their forces on the Dutch television market.[11] RTL was the biggest of the private broadcasters, with two commercial channels, Veronica the strongest of the broadcasting associations tied to the public

(*Municipality of Almelo* v. *NV Energiebedrijf* [1994] ECR I-1477). More recently, in the *Compagnie Maritime Belge* judgment (joined cases T-24/93,1996), the Court of First Instance saw joint dominance again within the meaning of Article 86 in the ties among ship-owners taking part in shipping conferences in which they agreed uniform hiring charges and contractual terms. As to the interpretation of the merger Regulation, the Court of Justice has now under review a decision of the Commission (Kali und Salz/MDK/Treuhand, n. IV/M.308, 1993) that is very similar to *Nestlè/Perrier* in imposing conditions upon a merger that would otherwise produce joint dominance. The Advocate General has already argued that only an amendment to the Regulation could allow the Commission to extend its powers to the prohibition of joint dominance.

[11] *RTL/Veronica/Endemol*, case No. IV/M.533, 1995.

networks, intending through the merger to move to commercial TV, and Endemol was the strongest of the independent programme producers. The Commission analyzed the three relevant markets separately—for television transmissions, advertising and independent productions—and compared the strong points of the new conglomerate with the situation of actual and potential competitors. On the transmissions market the new company would have integrated programming directed at the most numerous sectors of the public, attracted by the popular magazines in the hands of its shareholders and produced at lower cost than that of the public broadcasters, incapable of integrating and burdened with high staff costs; while the possible new entrant, the Swedish SBS, would have had only one channel against the three of the conglomerate. In this position the conglomerate, with its foreseeable 40 per cent, would have had a "very strong" position. On the publicity market, bearing in mind the legal restrictions imposed on public broadcasters and their difficulty in integrating and thus offering targeted advertising packages, the foreseeable quota, according to the Commission, was 60 per cent, the possibility of resisting any attack very strong and the position "dominant". On the market for independent productions, Endemol was already "dominant" (it already had the highest share, had exclusive contracts with many stars and was the only one able to offer the stars work in other branches of the entertainment business) and the merger would have strengthened it "with further negative consequences on small Dutch language producers survival chances". The parties offered to sell one of the two RTL channels, but the Commission replied that there was the "risk" of frightening an interested purchaser, because of the low competitiveness of that single channel. The merger was banned, and the case ended when Endemol dropped out of the arrangement.

The Commission's arguments were certainly reasonable

and internally consistent. Equally certainly, though, they were not consistent with the criteria of the previous decisions, and evidently inspired by further considerations: the coincidence in time with the Commission's own efforts to liberalize the telecommunications market and allow it to integrate with the television and computer markets in a framework of maximum openness; and the extra-economic concerns always present in legislation on television, aimed at guaranteeing a special pluralism there. It is certain that in this decision the usual boundary of bans on concentrations for lack of competitors, goes back to that of dominant positions still coexisting with competitors, with the likelihood, here, that others might enter (the Swedish SBS). The boundary in Regulation No. 4064 was, in short, being shifted so as almost to coincide with the one in Article 86 of the EC Treaty. In so doing the Commission was taking to extremes the view of greater efficiency not as an exemption factor but as a risk (this is particularly clear from the implicit treatment of the greater staff costs borne by public broadcasters as a "barrier"); it was protecting consumers not from market foreclosure and the associated restriction of output but from a restriction of existing pluralism, thus defending, along with their right to choose, the right to sell of the small producers currently on the market.

It is important to be clear on this, since it turned out—whether or not it was deliberate—to be the real significance of the case. But it is equally important to stress that it looks like a "single swallow that does not make a summer". The prevailing principle is the other one, which puts total market foreclosure immediately after the border generally accepted in merger bans; it is on these premises that it becomes possible to give the green light to mergers where commitments have been negotiated to make the market power not disappear but reduce to a level that can be "controlled" through repression of abuses. This once again confirms that the penalty for market power has not been abolished; but the "death penalty" is increasingly the exception.

### ANTITRUST AGAINST PUBLIC MONOPOLIES

One peculiarly European area of exception, the only one where the exception tends to become the rule, is the power of public monopolies or the holders of publicly-based exclusive rights. Towards these the Commission, and the Court of Justice itself, are markedly severe; indeed it is only towards them that the sanction of break-up, which in Europe is not directly provided for, has, indirectly, been applied.

So much severity in this sector is to be explained by the radical change in overall policies that there has been in the Community in recent years. Let us not forget that the EC Treaty, in Article 222 still in force, proclaimed its neutrality as regards the public or private ownership of enterprises. And Article 90 (2) exempted from the competition rules, and still does, all the activities of firms operating public services that are associated with and necessary to their task. To what is this change, and hence departure from the original spirit of these norms, due? There are several reasons: economic inefficiency as an ever more characteristic feature (even if not universal) of public enterprise, the increasing incompatibility of the single market with the compartmentalizing subdivision of national regulation of services rendered in each country by public monopolies, and technological development that has steadily undermined the basis for monopolies in several sectors (telecommunications, television, electricity generation).

The whole set of these considerations has permeated the approaches of the European agencies, which have embarked both on policies of liberalizing entire markets (with telecommunications the best known case) by regulations and directives and on specific actions opposing specific activities of the pre-existing monopoly enterprises, applying the competition rules. Against the background of the liberalization norms that were being adopted, these specific actions led both to progressive restriction of the area of the "tasks" providing exemption pursuant to Article 90(2), and to expanding the "abuses" of these enterprises to such a point as to regard as abusive not just this or that exercise of their exclusive rights, but their very existence.

On the first aspect, the point was reached in relation to a public electricity monopoly, of saying that the task of guaranteeing security of supply did not necessarily require a monopoly of the import and export of energy. These activities could accordingly very well be carried on in competition as long as this merely rendered the public task "difficult", whereas for prohibition the public task would have to have been rendered "impossible".[12] According to the celebrated *Corbeau* case,[13] the public task would have been rendered impossible by its financial impracticability should private parties in competition be allowed to "cream off" for themselves the more remunerative services, leaving the rest to the public operators. But collecting mail at home and delivering it rapidly, the Court decided in that case, is not likely to endanger the postal public service.

Still clearer are the cases of "abuse" involving the very existence of exclusive rights. The best known, and the most extreme one to date, is the *Höfner* case. What was at issue was the public monopoly of job finding in Germany, in the presence of private agencies that began engaging in it, at least for higher staff.[14] The employment office, though holding the monopoly, had done nothing to prevent the new (and illegal) competitors from finding a niche for themselves. But their illegality remained, and when the

---

[12] This is the *Almelo* case, cited in note 10 above.
[13] *Régie des Postes* v. *Paul Corbeau* [1993] 4 CMLR 621.
[14] *Klaus Höfner & Fritz Elsen* v. *Macroton GmbH* [1991] 4 CMLR 306.

case came before first the Commission and then the Court of Justice, both concluded that the office was unable to satisfy the whole of the demand, and that this lack, together with the legal bar on entry by possible competitors, constituted an abuse. It was quite true that the office had not manifested any intention in that direction; to the contrary. But abuse was and is an "objective" concept, manifested in this case through the joint effect of the "guiltless" behaviour of the office and the legal ban maintained by the State. The Commission, endowed with powers against either, had exercised them correctly by demanding the end of the abuse by ending the State measures permitting it.[15]

There was by no means negligible legal machinery at work in this decision. But readers will realize the overstretching of precedents it involved as soon as they consider the one the Commission availed itself of to support the abuse inherent in failing to satisfy the whole of the demand. For the precedent was a case where Volvo, which had secured copyright cover for spares for its cars, prevented others from producing them, yet left demand for them unsatisfied.[16] This sort of intentional behaviour, with manifest repercussions on prices, as well as on repair service times, was held to be an illegitimate use of intellectual property rights, even though these are something special; and hence an abuse (the relationship of which with the one by the German public employment office thus seems both undeniable yet slender).

The exceptional severity towards public monopolies, leading to decisions against them that would probably not have struck at private operators in similar circumstances, is not, then, a representative test for European antitrust

---

[15] Recall that by Article 90(1) of the EC Treaty, Member States must neither enact nor "maintain in force" any measure relating to public undertakings and undertakings to which they grant special and exclusive rights that is contrary to the rules contained in the Treaty (including those on competition).

[16] *A.B. Volvo* v. *Erik Veng (U.K.) Ltd.* [1989] 4 CMLR 122.

severity. Just because of its exceptional nature, due as we have said to policies certainly associated with competition but not coinciding with its rules, it confirms if anything another constant feature we have already seen emerging: European antitrust policy adapts over time to differing public policies. It had done so at other times, as we have seen, by shrinking; this time by expanding. In each case this brings out its twofold (and in part contradictory) role, as not just a system of balancing rules always remaining the same, but also a tool, a weapon, that can be turned to diverse ends.

# PART III

ANTITRUST
AND THE BOUNDS OF POWER

## PART III

ANTITRUST
AND THE BOUNDS OF POWER

# 7. DRAWING TOGETHER THE THREADS

### ORIGINAL AIMS AND LATER EVOLUTION

It is time to draw together the threads of this twofold evolution, in the USA and in Europe. The progressive emergence of new economic doctrines, new canons of interpretation, increasingly complex and sophisticated analyses, and persisting divergencies between the two sides of the ocean still do not eliminate one point in common: over the decades, the border marked in antitrust law to prevent transgression on economic freedom has been undoubtedly shifting forward. It no longer defends the freedom of small producers to stay in the market, it increasingly often accepts efficiency grounds for mergers, almost presumptively accepting them in the case of vertical agreements, and has consequently reduced *per se* illegality. In Europe, all this is topped with the two peculiar features due to the acceptance in principle of "some" economic power: the very notion of dominant position and the interferences from outside and inside of policies other than those on competition, which sometimes squeeze its rules and sometimes make them more flexible.

These are the points which have been reached to date. Can they be regarded as compatible with the original inspiration of antitrust? And if they are wholly or partly not, what is that due to? To the end of antitrust law in the fight against economic power, as Galbraith and Reich suggest, as we saw at the outset? Or to the end of the fight itself, which at least in the terms it was understood by the inspirers of antitrust law is now a matter of history? Or else to the change in the battleground, with the inevitable requirement it brings for other, different weapons that antitrust law, which performs a more limited function, ought not to seek to resemble?

## IN THE USA

In answering these questions, there has been much discussion in the USA on the reasons for antitrust law and in particular the objectives the authors of the Sherman Act had, a century ago now. As often happens with problems of this kind, today's advocates of opposing antitrust doctrines have found evidence of opposite intentions in Senator Sherman and his colleagues, and ended by attributing to those intentions an importance that they cannot have, at least in terms of the law and its present interpretation. In historical terms, in any case, it seems undoubtedly to be going too far to say that the Sherman Act was inspired by grounds of efficiency such as the Chicago School has focused on.[1] More reliable, therefore, seem to be those who trace antitrust law (as the Sherman Act was immediately called) to the fight against trusts, or against economic power, in defence of small producers and small traders who risked being crushed by it.[2]

In this direction too, though, there is a risk of going too far if that undoubtedly crucial moment is interpreted by making it the collecting point for all the threads of which American democracy is interwoven, even including some

---

[1] This was the thesis that made the publishing fortunes of R. Bork's *Antitrust Paradox*, cited in Ch. 1, n. 15 above.

[2] So, among others, H. Thorelli, *The Federal Antitrust Policy: Origination of an American Tradition* (John Hopkins Press, Baltimore, 1954); E. Fox, *The Modernization of Antitrust*, cited in Ch. 1, note 17 above at p. 1147; D. Millon, "The Sherman Act and the Balance of Power", in E. Th. Sullivan (ed.), *The Political Economy of the Sherman Act. The First One Hundred Years* (Oxford 1991), p. 85.

that in fact emerged years later.³ But it is indubitable that the chain that leads from the Sherman Act to the Clayton Act and the principles the case law took inspiration from in interpreting each can plainly be traced back to those threads, meaning that those who see antitrust law as a translation in early twentieth century terms of Jefferson's democratic ideals are right: a society of producers as far as possible equal among themselves and all independent of each other, so as to avoid the inequality of wealth and the disparity of power it entails, not only in civil relationships but in the relationship with political power itself, which may be corrupted both by the abuses of the powerful and by redistributive claims by the mass of dependent workers.⁴ Jefferson's small farmers had become Woodrow Wilson's "little men". It was in any case those that the Supreme Court was explicitly protecting in US v Trans Missouri Freight Association, by as we have seen condemning the railroad company's power to deprive the country "of the services of a large number of small but independent dealers who were familiar with the business and had spent their lives in it, and who supported themselves and their families from the small profits realized therein".⁵ And even decades later Judge Learned Hand would say (in *Alcoa Aluminum*) that:

> "it is possible, because of its indirect social and moral effect, to prefer a system of small producers, each dependent for his success upon his own skill and character, to one in which the great mass of those engaged must accept the direction of the few"

adding that this was "the purpose" of antitrust law.⁶

---

³ As perhaps D. Millon, cited in note 2 above, does. We have already mentioned in Ch. 1, note 7 above, Hofstadter's work, *The Age of Reform*, that reconstructs the contribution of the Wilson-period reformers to the Jeffersonian-type ideology reflected in the Clayton Act.
⁴ T. Jefferson, "Notes on the State of Virginia", Query XIX, in *Writings* (The Library of America, New York, 1984) p. 290.
⁵ See above, p. 11.
⁶ See above, p. 17.

In its initial approaches, in short, American antitrust law carries on its shoulders both the weight of economic efficiency and that of democratic efficiency, each equally identified in the dispersal of power, both in the market and in the institutions; on the explicit premise as regards economic power that it has no legitimation, since its very existence conflicts not just with efficiency grounds but with democratic principles. This was already said very clearly by Senator Sherman in talking about trusts: "if the concentrated powers of this combination are entrusted to a single man, it is a kingly prerogative, inconsistent with our form of government".[7]

## IN EUROPE

In Europe the differences are many. Suffice it to note that here Jefferson's dream of a society of citizens kept equal by frugal prosperity that does not become discriminating wealth and by the exercise of freedoms that do not become power did not generate liberal democracy, but the communist utopia, as the endpoint of a culture much more prepared than the American one to trust the State as a *deus ex machina*. However, the lack of legitimation of private power in a system with democratic roots (however democracy is understood) is a solid and at bottom obvious common premise. And when liberal culture managed to make its way among the meshes of the many varieties of European statalism and began to impose antitrust law (and not the State) as the means to combat that power, the similarities with the original principles of American antitrust law became considerable.

The story starts much later than in the USA. It was at the German university of Freiburg, as we have already

---

[7] I take this quotation from D. Millon, "The Sherman Act and the Balance of Power", cited in note 2 above at p. 111.

mentioned, that a group of economists and lawyers, subsequently called the "Ordoliberalen" and destined to exercise great influence in post-war Germany, laid down the premises for European antitrust law, linking them to the roots of liberal democracy. Already aware of the economic efficiency grounds to be found in various restrictions on competition (monopoly, they even said, is not necessarily inefficient), the ordoliberals set the reasons for antitrust law almost entirely in the area of the illegitimacy of private economic power and of the devastating effects it can produce. In so doing, not only did they express themselves in almost identical terms to Senator Sherman, but even took further steps that clarify the scope of these effects for both the democratic and the economic process.

From the first viewpoint they indicate that the overweening strength of economic power is not limited to generating undesirable collusions with political power (we have already mentioned that they had before them the most tragic climax to that phenomenon, the alliance between the "konzerne" in their country and the Nazi Government to first enslave and then exterminate the Jewish minority), but equally produces such divergencies in collective interests as to prevent the market economy from being a common identity matrix, thereby alienating the sympathy of the majority who thus locate their hopes outside it and indeed against it, and undermine the very roots of society itself. From the second viewpoint they put the stress on the need not just to avoid monopoly but in the first place to avoid the wars waged to conquer it, devoting enormous and often disproportionate resources to objectives and plans for concentration and thus distorting such fundamental institutions for economic relations as the contract: the contract, born as an expression of individual freedom and *ipso facto* a source of bonds that are and must remain the outcome of the consensus of each, instead becomes the vehicle of the power of the few and the servitude of others.[8]

How can all this be prevented from happening? It is here that the ordoliberals, firm supporters of the market economy, link up with the bases of liberal democracy and face its crucial dilemma. The market economy, they say, tends naturally to engender its monsters, and therefore has a need to be conducted within the framework of a legal order that lays down rules to prevent that. In this framework antitrust law is an essential aspect, but not the only one; for just as the formation of private power should be repressed and if possible prevented, in the same way public power should be delimited to prevent it from infiltrating the economic machinery, under its own steam or impelled by private interests, altering its natural functioning. It is, then, the public power that serves to restrain private power through antitrust law, but woe betide, says Franz Böhm, if antitrust law is so patterned as to make public power the interested mediator that now suppresses and now conciliates the interests of feudal magnates.[9]

## THE LIMITS TO ANTITRUST LAW

The awareness of the limits to antitrust law is, then, very much present to its conceivers and pioneers; to the Europeans just as it had been to the Americans, as shown by the dialectic, very vivid in the Supreme Court's first judgments, between defence of the right of the many, and the smaller, to be on the market and the risk of prejudicing, through bans on this or that contract, the freedom of trade. It is however a fact that both for its conceivers and for its pioneers, especially the Americans who were work-

---

[8] I here summarize the main passages of F. Böhm, "Democracy and Economic Power" in *Cartel and Monopoly in Modern Law*, Vol. I (Verlag C.F. Muller, Karlsruhe 1961), p. 25.

[9] F. Böhm, cited in n. 8 above at p. 43.

ing in the atmosphere of the early twentieth century, antitrust law ought to be faithful to that society of free and (as far as possible) equal human beings that was its basic inspiration, under the banner of dispersal of power. It is no coincidence that they held dear the right of each manufacturer or trader, however small, to sell, no less than the freedom of consumers to choose among different products and prices. Nor was it any coincidence that it was marked by a broad range of *per se* illegalities which by their very nature pick out a very strict boundary around economic freedom, which they enclose in definite contexts without even giving its holders the time to explain the reasons for what they are doing and accordingly with entirely preventive force: not just before the damage is done, but even in such a way as not even to allow the premises for it to exist.

Nor can it be said, as some do, that with this approach the original antitrust law was taking on tasks that did not belong to it, being "multi-purpose" because it considered not just or even primarily the economy, the market and its rules,[10] but no less social equilibria and the defence of freedoms and equality in the face of the political process, which is instead a matter for democracy and its rules. For it should not be forgotten that the economic doctrines of the time portrayed an almost total coincidence between competition and economic efficiency; and if they were innovative in relation to the previous approach deriving from the common law (breach of competition = breach of freedom of trade), this came about in the sense of extending the prohibitions, the very prohibitions themselves, to all cases in which, while there was no breach of freedom of trade, there was restriction of the "options" offered to the consumer by the market (price fixing). It should be added that the markets were at the time largely closed within

---

[10] This is the criticism that usually comes from the cultivators of efficiency in a mode of strictest fidelity to the Chicago School. See F. Jenny, *Competition and Efficiency* (1993 Fordham Corporate Inst. (B. Hawks ed.), 1994) p. 185.

national frontiers, so that dimensional growth behind those frontiers was not balanced by actual or potential outside competition. It should finally be borne in mind that many of the concentrations and restrictive agreements that then fell under the attention of the antitrust bodies were the ultimate outcome of bloody competitive wars, and presented as their sole grounds of efficiency the elimination of the "destructive effects" of competition itself; which outside the limited sectors of the public services was inevitably bound to clash with the convergent arguments of efficiency, economy and democracy, protected by the antitrust law of the time. Either concentrations were to be regarded as admissible because they were useful for the better performance of a universal service and/or because they came in natural monopoly markets (but in that case they ought to be subjected to special regulation to contain and discipline their inevitable power against users); or else that power was in any case improper, and then even if the attempt was made to give it the human face of reasonableness, antitrust law was not in a position to accept it, for reasons in which economic efficiency and democratic efficiency came together.

### FACING CONCENTRATED, COMPETITIVE FIRMS

When was it that things began to change? When, faced with the evolution of markets, their extension on the one hand and the increased sophistication of their mechanisms on the other, economic analysis highlighted further discordances between restrictions of freedom of trade (with which competition was originally associated) and the manifestations of market power, which however this time went in the opposite direction from the extension of prohibitions initially brought by the classical theory of Marshall. Let us recall the evolution that took place in connection with vertical integration. That certainly constitutes a restriction on the freedom of distributor or retailer, who is tied by the manufacturer to places where he can sell and the third parties he can sell to. On the basis of the original viewpoint in the common law, restraint was undeniable, and it may also appear so on the basis of Marshall's theory, since the attenuation or even disappearance of intra-brand competition reduces the options for the consumer, and in any case alters the free play of supply and demand. But, says economic analysis now, if one considers the market for that product, has power over it really been formed? Is it not instead the case that vertical integrations make the competition between similar products in different brands more vigorous and efficient, so that none of the competing producers really acquires market power *vis-à-vis* the others or consumers? Let us further consider concentrations in relation to the expansion of markets: broadening widens the range of competitors, and for each of them widens the area of confrontation. In this context, merging does not necessarily take those involved out of competition; on the contrary it may in several situations allow transaction costs to be reduced and economies of scale increased, so as once again to make competition more vigorous and balanced.[11]

These conclusions can hardly be disputed, and if the antitrust objective is to hinder market power, it must be noted that in these cases such power is not present, so that the rules leading to attacks on it must be reviewed: the *per se* illegality of restraints enabling manufacturers to influence the final sale of products now outside their legal

[11] The analysis of concentrations as efficient ways to reduce transaction costs is due not to the Chicago School but to Oliver Williamson, among the very few scholars of industrial economics whose method and results that School respected. Williamson, who took account both of the teaching of Ronald Coase, and of the lessons of Chicago themselves, developed his ideas in a series of articles that ran through the 1960s and 1970s. For our purposes here, the most interesting work by O. Williamson (whose *Markets and Hierarchies* we already cited in Ch. 1, note 16 above) might be *Economic Organisation* (Wheatsheaf Books, Brighton, 1986).

control disappears; correspondingly, protection of intra-brand competition as a co-essential component of competition as such reduces; and as regards concentrations, the boundary for the prohibition goes back to take account now of both present and potential competition.

There is, then, a retreat, though not, within these limits, any greater tolerance for market power. Yet there are victims, and this still leaves more than one mark on the previous scope of antitrust law. The first victims are the "right to sell" and "right to independence" of small traders, who drop out of antitrust protection because power over them is no longer seen as market power (except only the limited case of boycotting, not as such upheld by efficiency grounds). In economic terms the conclusion is, as was said, unexceptionable, but in ideal terms it shifts the original antitrust root context: it is no longer the shield of the Jeffersonian society of equals, supposed to be reflected in a market of operators all of equal strength and all independent of each other. The incidence and limits of competition have changed: it no longer needs either equality or universalized independence, and what a competitive market has to assure is that there is no absolute control by anyone and that the room to grow is consequently kept open for everyone.

But at this point there is another victim too, and this is antitrust protection equally secured against market power and against its projection into the political process. While as we have seen original antitrust law managed to provide it, and to be organically "multi-purpose", this twofold potential is now being lost: a big firm that does not have economic power over a market that has expanded beyond national limits may nonetheless have in the domestic political process that abusive power it was the antitrust objective to contain. Antitrust law that sets its limit and hence its prohibitions where economic power is formed in the new, larger markets fails to catch the political power that previously could be curbed by its own prohibitions. Continuing to be multi-purpose in the same sense now would mean keeping much more restrictive and preventive controls available over the formation of actual economic power than an increasingly robust and increasingly widely-shared economic doctrine is willing to admit.

## CHANGING MARKETS—WHAT REMAINS?

But the changes antitrust law has undergone go much further. They are due chiefly to the fact that the evolution of markets that has brought about its own evolution also includes, in very many sectors, the progressive formation of oligopolistic markets. It is this oligopoly that is the enemy that according to some is really pushing antitrust law "against the ropes", by making it unable to challenge not just the political aspect of economic power but even its direct manifestations on the market. We mentioned at the outset that J. K. Galbraith was already regarding antitrust law as outdated by the 1950s, since he felt it was too blunt in the face of oligopolistic power, which he thought could be better opposed through the balancing power of those directly interested against it, from workers employed by big companies to consumers of their products or services, to the savers buying their shares through financial institutions.[12]

The argument about "countervailing powers" is anything but irrelevant, and indeed plays a decisive part in the overall pattern of a democratic society. Is it really true, though, that these powers have supplanted antitrust law, and that in any case its role is exhausted? Answering yes would certainly be going too far, but answering no would in turn be too little. That antitrust law has no role in oligopolistic markets is refuted by the facts, and the various

[12] J. K. Galbraith, *American Capitalism*, cited in Introduction, note 2 at p. 130 *et seq.*

American and European precedents we have been able to cite. These precedents indeed tell us that it has gained renewed vigour from the struggle with oligopolistic markets, and has in some cases made its competitive standards more exacting: on these markets an agreement constantly to exchange information that in other situations would be regarded as lawful in the absence of explicit horizontal agreements on prices or market-sharing is instead treated as if it were itself an agreement on prices or market-sharing, and hence prohibited (at least in Europe; in the USA it must also be proved that its effect is to raise prices); while the exclusion of new entrants through exclusive distribution networks organized by each of the few occupiers of the market is treated as a concerted practice, illegitimate whenever the intention toward it and price raising can be proved.[13]

It is however a fact that on these markets the boundary between concerted practices and merely parallel behaviour, between agreements proper and unilateral opportunist responses to others' behaviour, is always very thin, therefore making the difference between prohibited anti-competitive conducts and conducts antitrust law cannot oppose very slender. It is inevitable that this should be so: oligopoly makes transparent to every operator what is unknown to the many operators on a more strongly competitive market; consequently it does not present the same risks, and it discourages competitive wars, because the costs they involve are *a priori* higher than the benefits they might bring on structurally stable markets. In short, it is a position where antitrust law can act as a restraint on some behaviour by the powerful who are its protagonists, but also takes note of what they are, namely the powerful. Here Galbraith hits the mark: to the extent that antitrust law is and aspires to be prevention of economic power, oligop-

---

[13] See above, p. 32.

oly is the proof that something has irreversibly slipped through its filters. Nor is the answer now prevalent among the American economists—that market power as closure of the market, and absence of any possible competition, with oligopoly has not necessarily come about—a tranquillising one. This is certainly true: but it is no less true that the oligopolistic firm is different from one blindly operating, guided by prices formed over its head by the interplay of supply and demand, in a competitive market. The oligopolistic enterprise has, in relation to its market, non-exclusive but incommensurably greater power: suffice it to note that it can increase prices with a reasonable expectation of being followed rather than opposed, and that when instead it cuts them it in general knows that it is not increasing its market share but following a common cost trend that allows a reduction with equal returns. In short, the oligopolistic scenario has stability features that are the outcome not of a perfect, democratic competitive equilibrium but of an equilibrium between areas of influence acquired and respected. The obvious consequence is that the more markets there are where the situation is like this, the more antitrust law is circumvented and restricted to a residual area: the margins are at that point what they are, and what antitrust law then does is to exploit all the potential they offer. In these circumstances no-one could ask it to do more.

However these conditions, though becoming increasingly frequent, are neither so generalized nor so inexorable as might have seemed to Galbraith a few decades ago. In the first place there is the high rate of innovation that has come about in recent years. It may unpredictably render the oligopolistic scenario more varied whenever one firm or another has anticipated this or that rising wave. Then, very often as a consequence of the same innovative process, there is the continued formation of new markets, for goods and for services, on which initially there is a plurality of operators, perhaps of greatly differing strength, whose reciprocal relationships are anything but fixed, and for reasonably long periods remain open to varying patterns. There are, finally, the globalization and hence expansion of geographical markets, which bring into competition with each other firms with radically different costs, and disturb unexpectedly the oligopolistic equilibrium with the arrival of new players around tables where the few players already there had for years been playing with open hands.

On these dynamic flows of events, antitrust law has thousands of times been called to "say its piece". It is here that the choice it makes, the interpretation it gives its own role, the principles it feels itself bound by, play a role that may be decisive for the future patterns these flows will lead to. Certainly its choices and decisions will be interacting with the real trends of economic processes, and among these there undoubtedly is and has remained the one towards oligopolistic closure of markets: but it is one thing if this trend is encouraged, and quite another if it is opposed. The opportunities that ensue are plainly different, and in a changing world, whether they are there and can be grasped by someone, or are not there at all, is bound to make a difference.

# 8. THE DILEMMA OF LIBERAL DEMOCRACY

## THE DILEMMA OF LIBERAL DEMOCRACY WITHIN THE DILEMMA OF EFFICIENCY

It is against this background that something many economists now look at with disdain, closed as they are in their technical elaborations of efficiency conceived entirely one-dimensionally (consumer welfare as non-restriction of output), re-emerges forcibly from the ancestral antitrust memory: should the formation of economic power be stopped before barriers to entry are so high as to foreclose the market? If it may be too late to intervene in the behaviour of operators now shut within the precincts of an oligopolistic market, can antitrust law influence the structure of such a market in time to prevent its turning into such a precinct? What is coming out again is, then, the crucial issue of the boundary and hence the risk to be run depending where it is set, the risk of "too much" public power or, contrariwise, "too much" private power.

The dilemma, as we said at the outset, has its roots in the very principles of liberal democracy, affecting first and foremost the interpretations and translations they are given. It is however wrong to think that antitrust law, now free of the initial, improper burden of democratic efficiency, guided by events and the refined doctrines of economists to pay attention to economic efficiency alone, is now immunized against that dilemma and consequently running along such well-defined tracks as to be sheltered from the choices it requires. The error lies not so much in the intervening awareness of the separation between democratic efficiency, which is actually beyond the direct antitrust horizon, and economic efficiency. The error lies in accepting as truth the one-dimensional economic efficiency mentioned earlier.

Why should only the restriction of output of a given product, such as to shift demand to second-choice products (to do which society is constrained to higher costs with poorer results), be economically inefficient? This certainly is inefficient, and an agreement or concentration leading to such a result should certainly be prohibited by antitrust law. But who says that "consumer welfare", the pillar of this notion of efficiency, amounts solely to not having to shift to second-choice goods, and is hence satisfied by a market where one or a few producers satisfy the demand for existing products, without output restrictions? Someone has rightly noted that "there is a strong tendency among economists to define welfare in terms of efficiency in doing accustomed things in an accustomed way".[1] But might not consumers regard as serving their welfare the diversity of sources of goods and services, the existence of diversified potential for innovation, as much room as possible for market dynamics that favour the new products not yet designed and ways of producing them not yet designed?[2] Can it be said that all this has nothing to do with economic efficiency just because it shakes up the antitrust views of those economists who feel safer with one-dimensional efficiency?

The truth is that there is no one single concept of economic efficiency: there are at least two, and their antitrust implications are in the main different. For those who

---

[1] J. Dirlam and A. Kahn, *Fair Competition: the Law and Economics of Antitrust Policy* (Greenwood Press, Westport, 1984) p. 14.

[2] This is the position of E. Fox, cited in Ch. 1, note 17 above. Today in the USA, Fox is one of the most vigorous supporters of the "expansionist" antitrust positions.

# THE DILEMMA OF LIBERAL DEMOCRACY 111

understand it solely and exclusively as non-restriction of output, almost all the "*per se*" illegalities—including price-fixing—might confidently be let drop, since it is better to verify from case to case whether the behaviour challenged leads to inefficiency, that is to those restrictions or not; and if it does not, it is needlessly "intrusive" to prevent it. For those who instead see it as the maximum possible opening of markets, the "*per se*" illegalities retain their significance, since they preserve that opening by keeping the likelihood of new access and more intense competitive dynamics higher. For the former, predatory prices are rarely illegal behaviour, since getting rid of existing competitors does not necessarily mean escaping all possible future competition. The latter instead raise the problem of the eradication of possible competition through "domino" elimination of existing competitors through predatory pricing, and hence regard it as an antitrust duty to break the sequence before it is too late. The former see very few barriers to entry, fundamentally only the imperfections of the financial market that prevent the new entrant from having resources for the necessary basic investments, for making a name on the market through advertising, and for building up a distribution network. The second put the stress on the time that in any case all that may take, and on the difference between reinvesting resources generated from ongoing activity and recourse to the market, with the problem of remunerating the money borrowed in the initial stage of the new activity; and hence see barriers in the height of the basic investments, in advertising costs in markets where there is consumer loyalty to brands, and in the omnipresence of the existing distribution networks. The former protect competition and not competitors, consumers and not weaker firms. The second think that to protect competition ignoring existing competitors may destroy competition itself and therefore maintain the old "right to sell", the right not to be shut down unless justified, under the protection of antitrust (which is somehow what Europe does, even though in its excessively regulatory manner, by imposing "special responsibilities" upon dominant firms).

As we can see, two different antitrust perspectives emerge from the two versions, and the difference always, and significantly, leads to the same aspect. The first is antitrust law that delays intervention to the last, leaving the market to provide as far as possible by itself for a definition of its own dynamics and its own equilibria: only imminent risk, with no alternatives, of output restriction justifies and permits intervention. The second is antitrust law that seeks to prevent that risk emerging and inserts itself more frequently and earlier into ongoing market dynamics, seeking to influence their structure. The first, in other words, sets the boundary of public power as far ahead as possible, accepting the risk of private power; the second does not accept that risk and instead more runs the risk of preventive intrusions by public power.

Over and above the technical points and economic and legal arguments that give shape to the two concepts, we can see that they very clearly reflect the dilemma of liberal democracy, which is and continues to be the dilemma of antitrust law itself. The certainty of the technicians, especially the economists, that the side they take is determined exclusively by the superior validity of the economic analysis they follow (and in the USA this is a deeply rooted certainty, that calls for boldness in some quarters to go against) is bound to break against the conscious candour of those in institutional roles who openly take their side: that was the case with Justice Scalia whose dissenting opinion in the *Kodak* case we mentioned some pages ago.[3] Let us recall that in it, adopting the more restrictive notion of market power and rejecting the position that Kodak had it in the market for repairs to its machines, Scalia maintained that

---

[3] See above, p. 29.

antitrust law ought not to deal with such questions since it would otherwise transform "a specialized mechanism for responding to extraordinary agglomerations of economic power to an all-purpose remedy against run-of-the-mill business torts". Here the underlying motives for a choice are stated with praiseworthy clarity: they spring not from the clash of opposing economic doctrines but from the whole set of values and complex reasons that lead each of us to take this side or that in the dilemma of liberal democracy.

## TOWARDS AUTONOMY OF EUROPEAN ANTITRUST FROM OTHER COMMON POLICIES

This conclusion, just because it does not allow one of the possible antitrust roles to be dubbed just but instead excludes there being only one, serves as such to clarify the reasons for the inevitable choice between them to anyone facing it. For just that reason it has especial value at the stage Europe's long antitrust evolution has now reached.

Ours has been an inexorably different evolution from the American one: not just for cultural differences, which even the spiritual fathers of our antitrust conceptions, the Freiburg Ordoliberals, sought to attenuate, but also and especially because of differences in time. For both reasons, a competitive market in the image and likeness of Jefferson's society of equals has never been pursued here. Not only were we historically accustomed and culturally not opposed to recognizing private power subject to its bridling and balancing through regulation and the direct entry of public power to the economy, but it is a fact that our antitrust law began when the oligopolistic structure of many markets was already a reality.

This set of circumstances has meant that our antitrust law was from the outset not a negation but a limitation of private power, and that from that viewpoint it combined two different natures: the classical "surgical" one, and an entirely European, markedly regulatory one—the acceptance of the dominant position as a position of independence from competitors and in any event something different from and less than total market closure, the special responsibility of the firm that holds it, and the treatment of various types of abuse, are perhaps the clearest examples of this European specificity. One should of course add another outcome of the same historical matrix, namely the sensitivity our antitrust law has always shown to the policies surrounding it: industrial policy primarily, but also regional and social policies, which now limit it on the outside (the free zones it tolerated) and now condition it from the inside (generosity in seeing "indispensable production improvements" in agreements or concentrations consistent with the aims of those policies). A mention should, finally, be made of the part played by the objective of market integration, which rigidified our case law in situations where the American brand was already much more flexible.

Given these premises and these contents, our antitrust law not only had different origins but a different evolution too from the transatlantic one. The core of our *"per se"* illegality was and has remained associated with market integration (consider the bar on any contractual limit to parallel imports) and hence has not suffered from the criticisms of those illegalities by the Chicago School: ours were at another level and have thus remained, so that they are still today a limit in the area of vertical agreements themselves, which are instead in the USA (as they otherwise are in Europe too) the restrictions on contractual freedom that least restrain competition. Again, our abuses of dominant positions express a lasting, unchanging severer antitrust orientation than the American ones, and no economic analysis has been able to modify or mitigate the "special responsibility" of firms which, surrounded by weaker competitors, are strongly restricted from conduct that in the USA would today be classed as "aggressive" competition. This means that by a long path that is all our own, and quite far away from the one that at the turn of the century set up the notion of efficiency on the other side of the Atlantic as openness of market processes, we have arrived at adopting one that has a similar aim regarding abuses and continue to be loyal to it, even assuming decisive regulatory nuances in doing so.

Conversely, when we move to the consideration of agreements, we first define as restrictive agreements that are so from the legal and contractual viewpoint alone, with no economic analysis of their actual competitive restrictiveness; then, when we move on to that analysis (which we do only in terms of exemption, balancing the restrictions against the efficiency grounds adduced by the parties), we are even more generous than one would be in the USA in recognizing the productive improvements resulting from the agreement, and the fact that it is necessary to securing them; which might please Justice Scalia, if it were not for the fact that we reach that point not from a convinced option in favour of non-intrusive antitrust law, but more often because of the influence of our industrial or regional policy. There is, finally, the vast case law on concentrations, perhaps the only area where we come closer to the notion of efficiency today most accepted in the USA, the one that sets the prohibition at the limit of restriction of output due to foreclosing barriers. But we are much more inclined to decree fore-closure in the presence of entry barriers that in the USA would instead be regarded as less than insuperable difficulties, especially when the merger concerns sectors where liberalization processes guided by the Commission are under way, so that there is a predominant political interest in shifting to the other notion of efficiency and hence moving the boundary of the prohibition further back.

Europe does not, then, present a linear picture. There are several reasons. Among these not the least are those associated with protecting market integration, or those going back to the acceptance, already there in the EC Treaty, of the dominant position. Consequently, the resulting rigidities are a fact that will remain in the European antitrust picture, irrespective of its greater or lesser consistency with the interpretive choices to which, from other viewpoints, its principles will remain subject. What ought instead to be dropped is interference in the antitrust area from policies of other types that have so far influenced it. From this viewpoint the times are, and are beginning to be seen as, ripe for attention to be paid (as has not yet been done) to the new framework set for us by the Maastricht Treaty. On the one hand there is the autonomy of the principle of protecting competition in relation to other principles and to the sectoral policies; on the other is the new conception it adopts of industrial policy, seen no longer as a derogation from competition but on the contrary as promotion of competitive markets.[4] From both directions, then, convergent indications are coming for a liberation of antitrust law from the multiple purposes it has served in the past, enabling it to be, as in the USA, antitrust law pure and simple.

The implications of this change (if it comes) may be manifold. The first and most general one ought to, and perhaps will, be if not the disappearance, then at least the weakening of the old regulatory propensity that has done so much to make our antitrust system a hybrid one and has found so much nourishment in the need to balance the protection of competition against other Community objectives. From this preliminary viewpoint, being antitrust and nothing more would mean being rooted

---

[4] We refer to Article 130 introduced as an amendment by the Maastricht Treaty, already mentioned in Ch. 3, note 7.

more in the encounter between freedoms and economic rights at stake from time to time, and less in the tradition of balancing varying public interests; and it would mean making economic analysis the yardstick for verifying in a specific case the extent of such freedoms and rights (and of any infringement of them), rather than being just one instrument for that balance among many. There would be important practical consequences.

The liberation of antitrust law from objectives extraneous to it ought, thus, to affect the present interpretation of Article 85, which is very rigid as far as the first paragraph is concerned, but often permissive as regards the third, and thus clearly reflects different kinds of logic from those intrinsic to a proper antitrust analysis. For whatever notion of economic efficiency one chooses to follow, if that is what antitrust law ought to refer to in judging whether an agreement is restrictive it is quite clear that the current interpretation of the first paragraph is not based on any economic analysis, since it stamps as restrictive agreements those that may well be so from a legal contractual viewpoint but might very well not be in relation to competition on the market. In this way, these agreements are automatically brought under the scrutiny of the third paragraph, following which they are sometimes, as we said, very generously exempted, but other times are exempted just because it is found they have no restrictive effects and perhaps even help to promote more efficient competition (as is the case for many vertical agreements). What, then, is the sense in finding exempt because it ultimately proves nonrestrictive an agreement that has been made subject to exemption procedure on the (necessary) premise that it was a restrictive agreement?

The contradiction is clear, nor are the legal pretexts supplied by the language of the first paragraph enough to explain it (it is true that section 1 of the Sherman Act was no less broad). It is in fact due to reasons that go beyond interpretive canons and doctrinal opinions and have to do with the pattern of powers and the interrelation among policies within the Community system. As is well known, national civil judges are empowered to give direct application to Articles 85 and 86 of the EC Treaty, if a private party approaches them for protection of rights against an agreement or a presumed abuse of Community relevance; and the national competition authorities themselves, where they exist, can do the same. What is manifest is that neither the judges nor the national authorities can make use of the power of exemption, which is regarded as a prerogative of the Commission because of its direct link with the unitary protection of Community principles and interests.[5] On that premise the Commission, simply because it is aware of the various grounds (not purely antitrust) that might make the balance go for or against exemption, wanted to extend to the maximum the relevant power, which thus includes those reasons themselves as well as those that lead to ascertaining not entitlement to exemption but the non-restrictiveness, in economic terms, of an agreement. In a climate, both national and European, where the boundary between antitrust policy and industrial and social policies was very fragile, this prevented national authorities and judges from being influenced by their respective country's industrial and social policies in declaring agreements of Community relevance restrictive or not, with grave impairment of the necessary uniformity. But the confusion it was intended to avoid at national level between antitrust, industrial and social policies was thus codified and took root at the Community level.

---

[5] The exemption declaration, issued by the Commission pursuant to Article 6.1 of Regulation No. 17/62, is regarded as a source of rights that the national judge too has to respect (*per* the Court of Justice in *N. V. L'Oreal and another v. P.V.B.A. De Nieuwe AMCK* [1980] ECR 3775). See also the "Notice on Cooperation between National Courts and the Commission", in OJC 39, 13 February 1993, para. 25.

Given that it is the EC Treaty that imposes the avoidance of any confusion and requires antitrust law to be antitrust law alone, it becomes even less tolerable for an economically non-restrictive agreement to be first found restrictive and then given an exemption. This implies bringing interpretation of the first paragraph to the canons of economic analysis already used, by the way, in relation to concentrations, means trusting to them and to rigorous respect for them to keep out extraneous policies, and redefining the exemption power accordingly as a power, certainly, but one transparently motivated by those (purely) Community policies that in particular circumstances may be held to prevail over an antitrust finding.[6] At that point, however, it will be clear that the agreement exempted is not and can never be a non-restrictive agreement, but is (and the Commission must assume the responsibility for this) a restrictive agreement permitted for other reasons (such as industrial, or social, or regional policy).

This is no minor change, especially because of the redefinition of the exemption power and the nakedness with which it exposes it. There is a rider, which may be still more explosive. If the antitrust verdict and the exemption measure are thus to be kept essentially distinct, one may ask whether they can both come from the same body, or whether the twofold role for which the Commission

[6] This theme is heavily under discussion today in relation to the decentralization of the Commission which it itself wishes to implement, to reduce its own workload by transferring decisions of lesser Community interest to the national competition authorities. Since it (rightly) wishes to reserve the exemption power to itself, it is clear that, at least as far as restrictive agreements go, decentralization would be illusory if the interpretation of Article 85(1) were to remain today's formalist one. For in this case the national authorities would be able to adopt very few decisions, since as soon as they felt they had to find an agreement restrictive they would be obliged to refer the question to Brussels, faced with the foreseeable request for exemption. On this point see E. Paulis, *Decentralisation of Enforcement of Community Law*, in C. D. Ehlermann and L. Landati (eds), *Robert Schuman Centre Annual on European Competition Law 1996* (The Hague 1997), p. 211.

would be called on would not generate an inevitable short circuit in it. For some time the proposal has been on the table to create an independent European competition authority. It is no coincidence that it came first from Germany (the fatherland of the Ordoliberals). The Commission is determinedly resisting, opposing specifically the reason behind the proposal: to separate the (political) regulatory powers from the decisional powers in the specific case, and place the latter in the hands of a non-political agency that would give guarantees of independence and respect for quasi-judicial procedures.[7]

As long as processes of liberalization are under way for purposes of which both regulatory and decisional powers in the specific case are being used in co-ordinated fashion, the Commission has grounds in its favour. But they are grounds that underline the continuing need to use antitrust law in a framework of principles and purposes that do not belong to it, to make it an instrument of broader policies. It is this which sooner or later must end, with all the consequences that may result. We have already noted that some of the more peculiarly European antitrust rules emphasize that it is founded not on the negation but on the acceptance of private economic power, which should nonetheless be controlled and limited. If on this premise an institutional pattern persists in which among the controlling and limiting instruments there is direct negotiation with the political and administrative power (it being nego-

---

[7] The pros and cons of the proposal are considered in C. D. Ehlermann, "Reflections on a European Cartel Office" in [1995] CML Rev. 471, where further references may also be found. One of Ehlermann's criticisms of the German proposal is that it would mean longer procedures because it provides that there could be appeal against the new Authority's decisions to the Commission. A proposal of its own has been put forward by the Italian Antitrust Authority, which avoids this criticism by providing only for appeal to the European Courts. On this see the Authority's own *Annual Report* on its activities for 1996, p. 11, and also A. Pera, *Reform of EC Competition Law*, (1996 Fordham Corp.Law Inst. (B. Hawks rd.), 1997), p. 000.

tiation that leads to mitigation both of the agreements and of concentrations to make them less restrictive, and since the Commission's nature is political and administrative), the whole antitrust story has to be seen as being set not in the context marked solely by the economic and legal bases that ought to be proper to it, but in those the Ordoliberals regarded as the most dangerous: the context, with its ever-shifting boundaries, of the relations of power, of the many and varied parties that may come around the negotiating table when the stakes are political, of the measuring of the result by the yardstick of the political consensus or dissent that might result.

It would be unfair to the Commission or to the history that lies behind us to see the European treatment of antitrust law solely and exclusively in these terms. Instead, in its procedural aspects, it reflects the same mixture there was in its underlying principles. For it is true that in time, especially recently with the impetus from the Court of First Instance, procedures before the Commission have become more and more consistent with due process principles, both of right of access to documents and right to oppose.[8] It is equally true that economic and legal arguments have weighted greatly in its motivation. The fact remains that the whole complex retains a highly hybrid nature, so that judicial review of decisions is compelled to take note that they are the outcome of political and administrative discretion. The judge consequently feels himself not competent to review the exercise of that discretion except for "manifest error", and the outcome is

---

[8] The Court of Justice itself had already, first in *Consten & Grundig*, then in *Hoffman-La Roche* (cited in notes 40 and 57 above) affirmed some strong points of the right to defence before the Commission, with particular reference to access to documents. Since then, as stated in the text, it has been mainly the Court of First Instance that has brought the topic under close scrutiny, to the point of affirming in *Solvay S.A. v. Commission* [1995] ECR II-1979, that the principle of "equal weapons" between the Commission and the enterprise concerned must be respected.

that the core of the decisions themselves—i.e. the reconstruction and assessment from economic viewpoints of the facts of the case—is subject only to that extremely limited residual control.[9]

This makes it difficult for an antitrust system designed to be primarily antitrust and no longer "multi-purpose" in the sense the term has been used in Europe (i.e. serving not just competition policy but also industrial, regional and social policy), to continue to be entrusted to the present institutional pattern. It could be, if the art of compromise, so essential to the survival and growth of the European institutions, leads to acceptance of further inconsistencies, with all the prices that of course have to be paid. But if the new premises are to be given their proper development, if antitrust law is truly to be freed from the interference that limits and conditions it, then the creation of an independent Authority to decide on restrictive agreements, abuses and mergers can be seen as the necessary conclusion, and the Commission will have to delimit its own space—on the one side as to regulatory powers, and on the other to the exemption power which it makes sense to keep under its prerogative, although limited to absolution (by way of derogation) of agreements that actually are restrictive.

At that point it is likely that our case law will in its reconstruction of the facts and in its economic analysis lose that "impressionistic" nature that some American critics have seen in it (which is the necessary outcome of the

---

[9] The principle that in relation to complex economic facts "judicial decision as to the legal description of the facts themselves should be confined to verifying manifest error of assessment by the Commission" was stated by the Court of Justice in *Re Remia BV and others* v. *Commission* [1987] 1 CMLR 1. It should also be said that since then its restraining role has perhaps been attenuated, and that judgments where the Courts cancel Commission decisions for manifest error have begun to change. See *Asia Motor France & Ors* v. *Commission*, 1996 ECR II-961 (T387/94) and *Société nationale des chemins de fer français & Ors* v. *Commission* (79–80/96) cases, both decided by the Court of First Instance in Autumn 1996.

# THE DILEMMA OF LIBERAL DEMOCRACY 123

weighing of manifold interests it is forced into today)[10] and acquire the analytical reconstructiveness and argumentative rigour that in part have already entered consideration of mergers, and are not wholly absent particularly in connection with agreements.

What we would, however, be wrong to expect (though some, from a comprehensible optical illusion, are beginning to expect it) is that at that point the uncertainties will disappear too: without the diverse options to choose among due to the political and administrative discretion in pursuing manifold public policies, there will be only the single, true solution required in each case by antitrust rules finally cleansed of all the rest. There are even those who cultivate an expectation of this kind but think of having a purified antitrust system that continues to be entrusted to the Commission. But even with the prospect of an independent Authority, that would be illusory. Certainly, the options deriving from the range of interests that today bear on the decisions will and would in any case disappear. What will not go are those ones inherent in the very principles of competition, deriving from the crucial dilemma as to the boundary between the risk of market power and the risk of intrusive antitrust measures. We have already seen how many aspects the dilemma affects, from the weight attributed to entry barriers to the room instead left for "*per se*" invalidity, and how different the prospects are according to whether all that is considered to be "inefficient" is solely ultimate market foreclosure, or else a non-open structure of the market itself. These diversities are not destined to disappear when industrial policy disappears from the antitrust area. They are not destined to disappear because they are inside antitrust law, and forgetting them and instead relying on certainties that can be acquired means yielding to the unconscious certainty of those

[10] P. Jebsen and R. Stevens, "Assumptions, Goals and Dominant Undertakings", cited in Ch. 5, note 4 above at p. 471.

economists who have no doubts as to the truth value of their concept of economic efficiency. And that would be an error. We have already said that truth does not lie in either the one or the other possible concept of efficiency. There is a choice that everyone inevitably has to make.

From a conclusion like this, we may be sure, some will draw arguments that if that is so, if not even antitrust law is sheltered from choices that have at bottom a political connotation, then it is useless thinking of independent authorities, so everything might as well be left with the Commission. That is not so. We have already seen the difference there is between the parameters for the exercise of political and administrative discretion by a structurally political body like the Commission, and those of judgment by an independent authority. Not seeing that, or regarding it as in any event irrelevant, is like using an axe in an operating theatre. That too would be a mistake.

## THE GLOBAL MARKET AND TOMORROW'S ANTITRUST

So we come to the conclusion. Antitrust law, born as a bulwark against the expansion of economic power in markets predominantly closed initially behind national frontiers (which was true not just one hundred years ago in the USA, but largely at the birth of European antitrust law several decades later) has inexorably had to undergo the consequences of the continued, steady expansion of the markets themselves beyond those frontiers. These consequences have to date been on the whole erosive, and have in different ways and aspects taken away much of its initial capacity for intervention.

Once the economic market has expanded in relation to each national political arena, extending competition accordingly to big companies of diverse nationality, it was inevitable for antitrust law to lose the role of antidote to the exercise of abusive political influence by them. To pur-

THE DILEMMA OF LIBERAL DEMOCRACY 125

sue democratic efficiency different remedies had and have to be sought from the antitrust ones which, at a now different level, can guarantee only economic efficiency: what was and is needed is the organization of other economic interests (employees, consumers, savers and shareholders) capable of giving rise to the balancing powers Galbraith spoke of; what is needed is the severe discipline of conflicts of interest so as to avoid at least the most direct mixtures between economic power and political power.

It was equally inevitable for the transformation of various initially fragmented markets into oligopolistic markets of large firms to result in the drastic limitation of the force (which still existed) of antitrust law in relation to those markets to the extent that they took on stability unaffected by any external dynamics. Finally, a further phenomenon was inevitable that we have not mentioned, namely that the growth in the size of markets would take outside of existing, national or (in Europe) at most Community, antitrust jurisdictions operations in restraint of competition in relation to which the power of each of those jurisdictions is consequently attenuated.

But before going further and considering all the consequences proper to this last phenomenon, we should nonetheless stress what is by contrast not inevitable: the limitation of antitrust that some see in the intervening refinement of economic analysis applied to it, which on this interpretation has even detached it from the question of economic power and rooted it in the soil of efficiency alone. This is not so. Antitrust law has in fact become better and stronger by becoming able (thanks to economic analysis) to distinguish between restrictions of contractual freedom and restrictions of competition. It becomes unilateral and questionable when, over and above that and irrespective of that, it attributes to objective reasons of economic analysis such a retreat in the borders of its own intervention as to ignore the economic power whose formation it allowed. This was and is not at all inevitable. It is on the contrary the outcome of a choice that some hide under technicalities and others reduce to a clear ideological approach: to regard both break-up and the limitation of private economic concentrations not as legitimate responses to abusive power but as abusive violations of individual freedom. This is of course legitimate, but it is neither true nor necessary.

Awareness of this is essential in order not to regard the antitrust chapter as closed in the face of ongoing changes, and to grasp not just the erosions but also the potential arising from these once it has been noted that markets are tending to become global. For it is quite true that none of the existing antitrust authorities is today capable of intervening, or at any rate of doing so adequately, in the face of operations that go beyond its boundaries. But this does not mean that there is no need felt for antitrust law, nor that, albeit under different impulses, ways may not be sought to raise intervention to transnational levels: sometimes, as is the case with less developed countries, to escape monopolization attempts by large foreign firms no longer held back by competitive barriers; sometimes, as with the USA, to protect national firms from discriminatory barriers erected against them on foreign markets through agreements between local firms; sometimes, as is increasingly frequently the case, to protect consumers in various national markets against worldwide monopolies or quasi-monopolies that no-one is able to oppose alone.[11]

Phenomena of this kind are, or at least may be the signs of a new era for antitrust law, called on to keep open world markets just as it previously was for national markets. But here the choice comes between the task to keep markets open, or to intervene only once they are almost definitively closed. If the latter approach is what one thinks cor-

---

[11] F. M. Scherer, *Competition Policies for an Integrated World Economy*, cited in Ch. 5, note 1 above.

rect, then the room for intervention on markets still exposed to thousands of currents like the global ones will indeed be reduced and the needs that can be responded to by antitrust measures will find other types of defences. Developing countries will go back to erecting commercial barriers because they will see antitrust law as a "license to kill" for foreign multinationals; the USA will seek to protect not competition, but their national firms, against anyone who places them, and only them, in any difficulty whatever. It is no coincidence that in the USA itself it is just those advocates of the most reductive antitrust concept that support further reduction of the barriers in favour of domestic firms coalescing against particularly aggressive foreign competition.[12]

From this viewpoint too, then, the challenge coming from globalization is crucial. As the Ordoliberals (but not just them) taught us, markets never live in a sort of state of nature, but the natural flows running through them always meet limits. Either these limits are imposed by the legal system for competition, or there will be limits of another kind, an expression of other systems, or perhaps of inexorable disorder. A century ago it was national markets that faced this dilemma: today the dilemma arises for the global market.

It will not be easy to tackle and solve it optimally. The attempts being made today number basically three:

(i) The first is unilateral extension of each jurisdiction, theorized in particular in the USA[13] and repeatedly

---

[12] See Th. Jorde and D. Teece, "Innovation and Cooperation", cited in Ch. 2, note 8 above.

[13] On the various stages in the establishment of this doctrine in the USA see E. Fox, "Toward World Antitrust and Market Access", in (1997) 91 *Am. J. of Int. Law*, 1, which is highly critical in this respect. It should be said that both Congress and the Justice Department are tending towards priority recourse to bilateral collaboration, as we shall immediately see, reserving unilateral extension as a last resort.

practised by others too, including Italy:[14] this has all the defects of unilateral actions (which by definition are never done by networks nor from a common culture) and also their limits, since it is effective only when there are ways of punishing the firms responsible with penalties.

(ii) The second is bilateral agreement between existing jurisdictions, such as today between the USA and the European Community, and between the USA and Canada, making it possible to investigate cases jointly, or at least to exchange informational and investigatory assistance.[15]

---

[14] Unilateral extension is somehow implicit in the European regulation on mergers, that provides for Community's jurisdiction on the pure basis of turnover (above a set threshold). The Commission has extended its jurisdiction also to agreements among parties that are established outside the Community, when the restrictive effects of such agreements occur in the Community (with the support of the European Court of Justice, as long as it is in the nature of the agreements to be "implemented" inside the Community: see the Wood Pulp Case quoted above p. 57).

The German Act Against Restraints of Competition explicitly states that "this act shall apply to all restrictions of competition occurring in the territory of the application of the act itself, even if they result from restraints conducted outside such territory" (Sect. 98.2).

Due to a national merger regulation similar to the European one, Italy extended its jurisdiction in a recent case, involving the privatization of the Bulgarian company Sody, that was to be acquired by the Belgian company Solvay (both companies having a turnover in Italy above the national threshold). The Italian Antitrust Authority imposed conditions on the merger, among which a request by Solvay and other European producers to the Community that was necessary to the effect of a quick removal of the antidumping measures protecting them from US competitors (see Solvay/Sody in Autorità Garante della Concorrenza e del Mercato, Bullettin, 15, 1997, p. 12).

[15] This is the principle of "positive comity", that the Congress itself has encouraged by the International Enforcement Assistance Act of 1994, following which the two agreements mentioned in the text were promulgated. The principle was codified in Article V of the Agreement between the European Community and the USA, in O.J. L95/45, 27 April 1995.

(iii) The third, more ambitious, one is to construct a shared antitrust code in a multinational context, applied by multinational agencies.[16]

Ultimately it has to be this third solution that is the most appealing, for various reasons, not least that it would best express the capacity for public institutions to follow (without hampering) the constant expansion of economic activities, which those very institutions have largely lost sight of since they broke out of the boundaries of nation states. That does not, though, necessarily mean that pursuing it today, in a world marked by different cultures and rooted sentiments of State sovereignty, will bring useful results. There are those who feel it would be much better to extend the network of bilateral agreements, giving the necessary time for building up joint principles with joint meanings, something we are still too far away from.

This is a topical debate that is destined to continue for the coming years. It is evidence of a history—the history of power and antitrust law—of which the first chapters are perhaps now being written. But we can already glimpse a future that is certainly unknown, but for this very reason open to the options and the dilemmas of yesterday and today.

---

[16] This is the scenario most favoured by the European Union, but the hardest to bring about, bearing in mind the persisting diversities of culture and language among the many countries that have to agree on it, as well as the stubborn problem of sanctions. See again the article by E. Fox, cited in note 13 above, which makes an intermediate proposal for gradually arriving at a multinational agreement, via progressive harmonization based at the outset on a very few essential common concepts.

It should be recalled that the "Havana Charter" drawn up in 1946 under United Nations auspices (but never adopted) contained a worldwide antitrust code. A group of experts appointed by the European Commission produced a draft in 1995, and the matter is the object of meetings and discussions both in the OECD and in UNCTAD.

# INDEX

abuse of dominant position:
  assessment, 67–9
  Clayton Act, 65
  collusion, 83
  concentrations, 126
  discounts, 72
  discrimination, 74
  duopolies, 84
  Europe, 114
  European Union, 65–91, 116
  exemptions, 118
  foreclosure, 81, 87
  market integration, 86
  mergers, 83–7
  monopolies, 69, 74–5, 88–91
  objectivity, 69–72
  parallel behaviour, 83
  predatory pricing, 71, 73
  prices, 66, 71, 73–5
  prohibitions, 82, 85
  public monopolies, 88–91
  relevant market, 67
  resale, 72
  special responsibility, 65–6
  types, 72–76
  United States, 65–6, 68–72, 76, 80–1
agreements *see also* Restrictive agreements
  bilateral, 128–9
  efficiency, 22
  illegal, 22
  market sharing, 106
  prices, 106
  reasonableness, 10
  specialisation, 63
  United States, 9–10, 34
antitrust authorities, 42, 122

Bellis, J., 79
Bodoff, J., 44
Bohm, F., 42, 100

Bork, R., 20, 96
brands, 25–9, 47–54, 103, 104

cartels:
  costs, 22
  Europe, 40
  European Union, 44
  illegality, 28
  Nazis, 40–1
  prohibitions, 15, 42
  restrictive agreements, 58
  trusts, 8
Chicago School, 20–7, 31, 37, 80–1, 96, 114
Clayton Act, 15, 19, 35, 65, 97, 103
Coase, Ronald, 103
codes, 129
collusion, 16, 83, 99
combinations, 9, 10, 11
Common Agricultural Policy, 44, 62
concentrations, 22, 102–5, 119, 126
concerted practices, 46, 106
contracts *see* agreements, freedom of contract
costs, 32, 71, 73

democracy *see* liberal democracy
developing countries, 127
Director, Aaron, 20, 21
Dirlam, J., 110
discounts, 72
distribution, 25, 48–9, 106
duopoly, 84

economic theory, 13, 24–5
efficiency:
  agreements, 95
  consumer welfare, 110
  economic, 110–11, 117, 124–5
  liberal democracy, 109–29

# INDEX

mergers, 95
  United States, 96, 98, 115
Ehlermann, C.D., 45, 120
Europe, 39–91, 98–100 *see also* European Union
  abuse of dominant position, 114
  antitrust authorities, 42
  autonomy, 113–24
  cartels, 40, 42
  collusion, 99
  contracts, 99–100
  discrimination, 98
  early development of antitrust law, 41–3
  Freiburger Ordoliberalen School, 40–1, 98–100, 113, 120–1, 127
  Germany, 41–2, 99, 120
  industrial culture, 39–40
  Italy, 42–3, 128
  liberal democracy, 98–99
  prohibitions, 42
  protectionism, 39–40
European Union, 43–77
  abuse of dominant position, 65–91, 116
  autonomy, 116
  cartels, 44
  Commission, 44, 122–4
  Common Agricultural policy, 44
  direct applicability, 118
  market integration, 44–5
  Treaty of Rome, 43
  Treaty on European Union, 45
evolution, 95–6

foreclosure, 81, 87, 109, 115
Fox, E., 7, 23, 32, 33, 34, 96, 110, 127
franchising, 25–26, 50–1
freedom of contract, 9, 99–100, 125
  restraints on trade, 12, 13
  Sherman Act, 11–12
  United States, 100–101
Freiburger Ordoliberalen School, 40–1, 98–100, 113, 120–1, 127

Galbraith, J.K., 1, 94, 105, 106, 107
Gerber, D., 41
Germany, 40–2, 99, 120
Gyschen, L., 66

Halverson, J., 32
Handler, M., 8

Harvard School, 16, 19
Hawks, B., 32, 66
Heidenhein, M., 40
Hofstadter, R., 15
Hovenkamp, H., 8

illegality:
  agreements, 22
  cartels, 28
  freedom, 101
  market integration, 114
  mergers, 95
  price-fixing, 26, 28, 111
  reasonableness, 27
  restraints on trade, 103
innovation, 23, 61, 101, 107
Italy, 42–3, 128

Jacquemin, A., 80
Jebsen, P., 70, 123
Jefferson, T., 97, 104, 113
Jenny, F., 81, 101
Jorde, Th., 32, 127

Kahn, A., 110
Kattan, J., 23
Korah, V., 66

Landes, D., 39, 40
Laslett, Peter, 3
liberal democracy, 2–4, 98, 109–29
Locke, John, 3

market:
  abuse of dominant position, 67, 86
  agreements, 106
  changing, 105–8
  geographical, 108
  global, 124–9
  integration, 86, 103, 114, 116
    European Union, 44–5
    illegality, 114
    restrictive agreements, 49, 52, 58
  oligopolies, 56, 105–8, 125
  pluralism, 14–19
  power, 24, 30, 32, 103, 104, 107
  prohibitions, 101–2
  relevant, 59, 61, 67
  United Sates, 107, 126
market pluralism, 14–19
Marshall Principles, 13, 102–3

## INDEX

mergers, 15–16
  abuse of dominant position, 83–7
  authorisation, 35
  efficiency, 95
  illegality, 95
  numbers, 34
  prohibitions, 15
Millon, D., 96, 97, 98
monopolies, 17
  abuse of dominant position, 69, 74–5, 88–91
  attempts, 34
  public, 88–91
  tie-ins, 20–21
  United States, 14
multinationals, 127, 129

Nazis, 40–1, 99
North, D., 23, 39
Nugent, N., 44

oligopolies, 56, 105–8, 125

parallel behaviour, 83, 106
parallel imports, 51, 114
Peacock, A., 41
Pera, A., 120
Pooling, 7
Posner, R., 20
power:
  circumstantial, 30
  countervailing, 105–6
  economic, 104–5, 109, 113, 124–6
  Europe, 40–1
  industrial, 118–19
  legitimate, 3
  liberal democracy, 2–4
  market, 24, 30, 32, 103, 104, 107, 112, 126
  political, 99; 104–5
  private, 4, 30, 40–1, 100, 113
  prohibitions, 104–5
  public, 30, 41, 100, 112, 113
  social, 118–19
  United States, 107
prices:
  abuse of dominant position, 66, 71, 73, 74, 75
  agreement, 106
  costs, 32, 71, 73
  discrimination, 15
  excessive, 66, 74, 75
  fixing, 9, 13, 26–7, 31–2, 35, 54
  illegality, 25, 28, 111
  parallelism, 57–8
  predatory, 21, 23, 71, 111
  reasonableness, 17
  resales, 27
  restrictive agreements, 54
  Sherman Act, 13
  United States, 9, 13, 15, 17, 71
prohibitions:
  abuse of dominant position, 82, 85
  cartels, 15, 42
  concentrations, 104
  market, 101–2
  mergers, 15
  power, 104–5
  United States, 14–19
protectionism, 39–40
public monopolies, 88–91

quality, 23

Reich, R., 1, 95
repairs, 28–30
resale, 25, 27, 72, 103
research and development, 32, 61
restraints on trade, 7–9
  freedom of contract, 12, 13
  illegality, 103
  reasonableness, 12
  Sherman Act, 10–13
  United States, 127–8
restrictive agreements:
  brands, 47–54
  cartels, 58
  Commission, 47
  concerted practices, 46
  definition, 115
  distributions, 48–9
  efficiency, 58–60
  European Union, 9–10, 34, 46–64
  exempted, 46–7, 51, 53–54, 59, 61, 63–4, 117–20
  franchising, 50–1
  horizontal agreements, 54–64
  innovation, 61
  market integration, 49, 52, 58
  market-sharing, 56
  oligopolies, 56–7
  parallel imports, 51

# INDEX

price-fixing, 54, 57–8
reasonableness, 46–7
relevant market, 59, 61
research and development, 61
specialisation, 63, 64
United States, 46, 53, 58
vertical, 47–54
wars, 102
Rockefeller, J.D., 8
rule of reason, 11–12

Scherer, F.M., 65, 126
Schneider, H., 40
Sherman Act, 7–8, 10–14, 40, 46, 96–9
combinations, 11
economic theory, 13
freedom of contract, 11–13
interpretation, 10–11
price-fixing, 13
reasonableness, 10–13
restraint of trade, 10–13
rule of reason, 11–12
small firms, 15
spare parts, 29
Stevens, R., 70, 123
Stigler, G., 20
Sullivan, L., 6, 33, 34, 96

Teece, D., 32, 127
Thomas, R.P., 39
Thorelli, H., 96
tie-ins, 16, 20–1, 30, 32
trusts, 8

United States, 7–36, 96–98
abuse of dominant position, 65–6, 68–72, 76, 80–81
agreements, 9–10, 34
antitrust, 7–19
brands, 25, 26–30
cartels, 8, 15, 28
Chicago School, 20–7, 31, 36, 96, 114

Clayton Act, 15, 19, 65, 97
collusion, 16
combinations, 9–10
concentrations, 19
costs, 32
distributors, 25
efficiency, 96, 98, 15
foreclosure, 115
franchising, 25–6
freedom of contract, 9–10, 100–1
Harvard School, 16, 19
illegality, 27–8
leverage, 16
market pluralism, 14–19
market power, 107, 126
mergers, 15–16
monopolies, 14, 17
New Deal, 24
pooling, 7
prohibitions, 14–19
prices, 17
 discrimination, 15
 fixing, 9, 27, 28, 31–2
reasonableness, 27
repairs, 28–30
resale, 25, 27
research and development, 32
restraints on trade, 7–9, 127–8
restrictive agreements, 46, 53, 58
Sherman Act, 7–8, 10–14, 96–7
small firms, 15
spare parts, 29
Supreme Court, 24–7
tie-ins, 16, 30, 32
trusts, 8
unfair competition, 14–15

Van Bael, I., 79

wars, 102
Willgerodt, H., 41
Williamson, O., 23, 103